MY LIFE IN GOD'S HANDS

WESLEY WATTS

My Life in God's Hands

This book is written to provide information and motivation to readers. Its purpose is not to render any type of psychological, legal, or professional advice of any kind. The content is the sole opinion and expression of the author, and not necessarily that of the publisher.

Copyright © 2020 by Wesley Watts.

All rights reserved. No part of this book may be reproduced, transmitted, or distributed in any form by any means, including, but not limited to, recording, photocopying, or taking screenshots of parts of the book, without prior written permission from the author or the publisher. Brief quotations for noncommercial purposes, such as book reviews, permitted by Fair Use of the U.S. Copyright Law, are allowed without written permissions, as long as such quotations do not cause damage to the book's commercial value. For permissions, write to the publisher, whose address is stated below.

Printed in the United States of America.

ISBN   978-1-951913-49-6   (Paperback)
ISBN   978-1-951913-50-2   (Digital)

Lettra Press books may be ordered through booksellers or by contacting:

Lettra Press LLC
30 N Gould St. Suite 4753
Sheridan, WY 82801, USA
1 303-586-1431 | info@lettrapress.com
www.lettrapress.com

PREFACE

GOD IN MY LIFE

As I sit here in the eighty-fifth year of my life, I think back over the years, and I ask myself, What have I ever done that God would bless me as he has? Well, I don't have a clue except for something a pastor told me a long time ago. He said, "Wes, the only way that the other people will know what God has done in your life is if you tell them. "So let me take you back as far as I can remember. As the song says, "Let start at the very beginning."

CHAPTER 1

On February 13, 1932, I was delivered at the Union Memorial Hospital on the Thirty-Third Street in Baltimore, Maryland. When my mother was able, she wrapped me in a blanket and took me to a house on Bartlett Avenue. When we arrived, my mother removed the blanket and handed me to my grandmother. My grandmother took me in her arms, looked at me, and made this statement, "This is the most beautiful baby I have ever seen!" (See the picture on the next page.) Grandmother took care of me because my mother and father worked together at a bookbinding factory in Baltimore's Inner City.

Two years later, my mom went to the same hospital, and when she came home, she brought a baby sister with her. Her name is Loretta. Now the house we lived in then was small, and after ayear or so, we moved to a larger house at 1130 Homestead Street. The house we moved into on Homestead Street had on the first floor a living room, a dinning room, and a kitchen with back door leading into a small fenced yard. The second floor had three bedroom, a bathroom with a window in it, and a small closet for storing things. There was also a cellar with a coal furnace, double washtubs by the back door that led into the backyard, and at the front part, a coalbin with a small window where coal could be delivered from the outside. The family consisted of Grandmother (Cathren), Grandfather (Peter), three uncles (Roy, Dan, and Jack), Dad (Samuel Wesley), Mother (Mildred), and my sister (Loretta). Things were pretty nice.

CHAPTER 2

Grandmother Birch had a large family. Besides the three uncles that lived with us and my mom (Mildred, she had three other daughters that were married and had children of their own. They are Annamay, Dolores, and Virgie. As I grew up, they all became important in my life.

Now I was five years old, and I used to ride my tricycle up and down the hill, which was just up the street from our house, down to the filling station that was almost at the end of the street. Now the number of the house we lived in was 1130 Homestead Street (remember that number it becomes important later). As I did sometimes when I pulled into the gas station, I would pretend to put gas into my bike. One day when I was doing this, I heard a word—"wait." I looked around but saw no one. Now I rode my bike back and forth a lot but never heard that word again.

One day while I was riding my bike up and down the hill, a little girl yelled from across the street. She said, "Hi, little boy, would you like to come to my tea party?"

I yelled, "I have to ask my grandmother."

So I did, and she said it would be OK but to let her make sure no cars were coming. I crossed over, and the little girl told me her name was Marie and she lived in the house numbered 1933. She also said that there was another little girl that lived upstairs that was coming to her tea party and that her name was Colleen. (Don't forget that name. It is important later.) We had lemonade and cookies that Marie's mother had made for Marie's tea party. After that- and for quite a few days after in addition to the tea party-the girls taught me how to play jacks. Colleen drew a hopscotch on the pavement. They also tried to teach me how to play jump rope, but both my feet would not come off without me falling down. They still won't!

Then something completely unexpected happened. A large truck was parked in front of Marie's house, and the men put furniture in it. And then they drove away. Shortly after a car stopped, blew its horn, and a lady came out with a baby in her arms followed by four girls. They got in the car and drove away. Colleen was gone without even saying goodbye. Two weeks later, another large truck was parked in front of Marie's house, and furniture was loaded into the truck. A car pulled up behind the truck. A lady and Marie came out, got in the car, and drove away. Gone. My whole world was destroyed. I found some boys that hung our by the confectionary store, and we all strated to play together.

Time went by. My mom wanted to get me enrolled in school. She took me around to St. Bernard's School that was on the corner of Gorsuch Avenue and Independence Street. Next to the school was a church, and on the other side was the place where the priest lived. Across the street was a grocery store with a small house next to it, and then there was the convent where the Catholic Sisters of Mercy lived. That is where Mom took me. She rang the doorbell, and someone in a long black dress with her hair and the top of her head covered answered the door and invited us in.

We sat down in two chairs that were in a small room, and then another lady dressed the same way came in and introduced herself as Mother Superior. I noticed when she came in that she had a wide black belt around her waist, and one end almost went down to the floor.

Mom and the principal talked. The principal told Mom that because my birthday was in February, the school year was almost over and I would have to wait till the following September to start school. I was relieved because of the strap that the sister carried. She also told Mom that she noticed I was left-handed and they would have to teach me to be right-handed. Mom and I left. Mom was disappointed; I was relieved. I had one more year before I was going to be going to school.

Well, summer came, and I made friends with two boys named Billy and Tommy. They lived next door to a a girl named betty, and we would play cowboys and Indians. Sometimes they would come down to my house, and we would use the concrete railings around the porch. It was about this time that Mom and Grandmother had the picture on the next page taken of me. I met a couple of boys that lived on Gorsuch Avenue named Burette and his brother, who became my best friend. Summer came to an end, and before I knew it, it was time to start school.

CHAPTER 3

Now I had not thought anything about God. In fact, I did not know who or what he is. Mom used to take me to church once in awhile, but not regularly.

On the first day of school, Uncle Jack walked me up the street, around the corner, and across Gorsuch Avenue along the side of the church to the back of the school. That is where the entrance was. All the kids-small ones like me (although I was big for my age)-were walking around talking, kicking a soccer ball around, and suddenly a bell went off. It was 9:00 a.m., time for school to start.

The first thing we did was to get in a straight line, and then the sisters marched everyone to their classrooms, starting with eight graders and going down to first graders. After we went into the classroom, the sister in charge assigned each person a desk and said that would be each person's desk for the whole year. There were boys and girls in the same class. Because everyone who started school that year was six years old and I was seven and taller, the sister put me toward the back of the room. We were taught the basics-prayer, learning to count, learning the A-B-Cs-just the basics. By the end of school year, I was no longer left-handed. Through many cracked knuckles I had learned that there were no left-handed people in that school. Things went pretty well during the first year in school, but now summer vacation was starting in June.

That summer was different. I had made some new friends to play around with during vacation time. I spent a lot of time playing cowboys with Bobby and Tommy, my cousins who lived on Montpilier Street, because there was a big lot there that we could play on. In the evenings, after dinner, I was allowed to stay out later, sometimes until dark.

One day, over on Gorsuch Avenue, a house had been torn down, so of course, my friend Ken and me and three others had to see it. We all explored. There was a big hole in the ground where the cellar used to be. There were some boards with nails in them still lying on the ground. Naturally, I found one of the boards. I had on a pair of tennis shoes and put my foot over the nail so none of us would step on it. We stood there looking into where the cellar was, then decided to go to the park and play baseball. Naturally, as we started to walk away, I stepped, and the nail went through the sole of my tennis shoe. When I found out that my foot wouldn't move, I called for help. Two of the gang held me up while Ken pulled on my left leg to get the nail out of my foot. We left the old torn-down house and started to go to the baseball field. But as we walked, my foot felt very wet. Plus, it felt like it was sticking to my sock. I told the guys I was going to go home instead. After some insults like "baby," "chicken," and "sissy," I hobbled away, walking and hopping to the house, up the front steps, and into the house. My mom and dad were both home that day as it was a Saturday. Mom sat me in a kitchen chair, lifted my leg to where she could see the bottom of my shoe, and then screamed and yelled to my dad to come and see. Dad came into the kitchen, took a look at the bottom of my shoe, and told Mom to get a towel and wrap it tightly around the shoe with my foot inside. Mom did as Dad said. He picked me up and carried me to the front door and yelled for Grandmother to open the front door. He yelled to Mom to open the back door of the car and then laid me down on the back seat. He and Mom got into the car and drove me to Union Memorial Hospital, which was only five blocks away.

When we got there, Mom ran inside. Two men and a wheelchair came out with her. They took me off the backseat, put me in the wheelchair, propped my left leg up, and ran into the hospital. When the doctor who treated me came to talk to Mom and Dad, he said, "He will be OK, but it is a miracle he did not bleed to death before you got him here." (Miracle, yes, because God wasn't finished with me yet.) Mom and Dad took me home after a nurse showed them and me how to use a set of crutches. The nurse told Mom to remove the bandage after two days, blot away with peroxide as much of the dried blood as she could, rebandage the wound, and bring me back in ten days to have the stitches removed. It turned out to be a very short summer vacation that year.

September arrived, school reopened, and I entered the second grade.

The teachers still had to remind me to write with my right hand. Their long black straps that hung at their sides and a yardstick made of wood were good reminders.

We learned some new things in second grade like the Lord's Prayer, had a book called a Catasambe, and had more reading, writing, arithmetic, and history. Religion and history were my two favorite subjects. Second grade came to an end, and again, it was playtime. During the summer, when I was rushing around home to hurry and get outside, I went to get something (I don't remember what is was) out of the cellar, opened the cellar door, missed the first step, and fell all the way down the steps. Grandmother was at the top of the steps screaming, "Are you all right?"

I said yes, but when I tried to stand, I could not put any pressure on my left leg. I crawled up the steps and sat on the couch in the dining room with an ice pack on my left ankle. When Mom and Dad got home, I told them what happened. Again, Dad carried me the car. Into the back seat I went, and once again, we were off to the hospital. Dad drove to the emergency door side; Mom went inside and came out with wheelchair and an attendant to help me into the chair. After some x-rays, a broken ankle was the prognosis. Two hours later, after the plastic brace had been put on my left foot and leg, we started home with another pair of crutches.

That summer was also cut short.

CHAPTER 4

Well, my third year of school was about to start. I was now nine years old. I had grown very tall over the summer, and when the other kids showed up for school, I was the tallest kid in the whole room. For some reason this year, before lessons started, a priest from the church would come into the classroom, whisper something to the sister, and then he would say a prayer. He would lead us in the Lord's Prayer and the Pledge of Allegiance to the American flag, then he would leave and the sister would begin the lessons.

Time passed, and school closed for summer vacation. Again, I was off and running with the crowd. Somehow I had really gotten into going to the movies on Saturday morning. At 10:00 a.m. when the movie opened, there I was in the line with fifteen to twenty two-gun packing cowpersons (boys and girls) ready to help Gene Autry, Hopalong Cassidy, the Durango kid, and of course, my favorite cereal-the Lone Ranger. With my twenty-five cents allowance, I had ten cents to get into the movie, five-cents for a box of Good and Plenty, and another five cents into the vending machine for a box of fruit juice. With my two cap pistols at my sides, just in case any of my heroes needed help, I was ready.

One Saturday after the movies, instead of going to the park behind the school, I dediced to go home. Why, I don't know. My dad was sitting in the dining room, puffing on his pipe and reading the newspaper. He looked at me and said, "What ya doing?"

I replied, "Nothing."

Then he took me completely by surprise when he said, "How would you like to go to the rodeo with me?"

I was shocked. "Really?" I replied.

"Really," he said.

Up to this point in my life, I thought my dad really didn't like me.

I was only there because my mom and grandmother wanted me there. "When?" I shouted.

"Right now," he said. And he took me by my hand, and we walked out the front door, down the steps, up the street, past the school and church, and over the big lot where we kids usually played (but for some reason, I did not know it was filled with cars). Then I saw it-the Baltimore Memorial Stadium. We walked up to the gate, and there were two men taking tickets from the people as they went in. after they took the tickets, they said, "Enter at the left." When Dad handed our tickets to the man, he looked down at me and said, "Enter to the right." We followed his order, and when we entered into the stadium, there was this man dressed like a cowboy who was putting a saddle on a horse.

The man turn around, looked down at me, and said, "Howdy, buckaroo, my name is Gene Autry. What's yours?"

I stood there dumbfounded. Dad said, "Aren't you going to shake hands with Mr. Autry?" I stuck my hand out.

Gene shook hands and said, Hey! How would you like a little ride on Champion?" I don't remember ever answering him. Gene reached down, picked me up, put me in his saddle, and walked Champion around, with me on his back, in a circle under the stands. That was a moment I will remember all my life.

Gene brought me back, took me of Champion, and handed me to my dad. As Dad was holding me and as I was shaking like a leaf in a windstorm, Gene took my hand and, while shaking hands, said, "Gotta go. Got a show to put on. Nice meeting ya." And then he rode off into the center of the stadium. It was another moment I will never forget. It was the first time I felt my dad really loved me.

CHAPTER 5

School opened, and everything was set to go. All the people who were in the first and second grade were in the classroom. We all seemed pretty happy to be together again. I had grown quite a bit and was still the tallest kid in the class. So I started to slide down on the chair so my head was almost as low as the other kids. As the year went by, at some time, we were given report cards to take home and give to our parents to read, make written comments on them, and sign them. Then we were to return them to the sister for next quarter. My best subjects were still religion and history. Unfortunately, reading, writing, and arithmetic are the subjects that knowledge is based on.

Now while I was left-handed, I had good writing skill, but learning right-handed, I went from B+ to D and, for some reason, never did learn to write. Spelling was another thing I could not seem to understand. You see even today I spell everything the way it sounds. I always thought while I was in school that I would never get a job that arithmetic would ever be used in. (Boy, was I mistaken.) so when school was about half over, I was given a note to take home. The head sister wanted to have a talk with Mother and Fatherat their convinience. Well, we all met with her, and she told them that I was in danger of failing, and if I did not bring my marks up, I would have to repeat the third grade. Well, I really tried studying hard, doing my homework and turning it in, and praticing my writing. My marks got better, and at the end of the school year, I was able to pass with a C+ average.

School was over, and summer was here again. Now during the school year, we were required to go to church on Sunday for the nine o'clock mass and had to sit with our school class. In the summer, when school was out, we could attend any service we wished. This year on Sundays, we would load up the trunk of the car with food and drink, then Grandmother, Mom, Dad, Loretta, Grandfather, and I would get in the car and head for Rocky Point. We would leave home in the morning on Sunday, drive to Rocky Point Park, park the car, and carry our ice chest full of beer and soda and our picnic baskets full of sandwiches, fruit, and maybe sometimes cake or pie. We would swim all day, or sometimes Loretta and I would be allowed to play bingo. Oh, the good old days of bygone summers.

Time passed, fall came, and before I knew it, back-to-school time was here. Now I was ten years old when I started the fourth grade. I did not really have much interest in school that year I thought that I knew enough. But I really got interested in church. I wanted to be an altar boy. I thought that if I could be an altar boy, schoolwork would be easy. That did not work. The priest said that to be an altar boy, I would have to be twelve years of age, have good attendance in school, and hold at least a B average in schoolwork. But they would not even consider me even if I met all of the requirements. My bubble was busted. My marks in school dropped, and by the time school closed, I had failed the fourth grade. Summer of this year would be different, I thought. *I'll get a job and show them education doesn't count,* I thought.

one Saturday I took my little red wagon around to Greenburg's grocery store and sat. when the ladies came out of the store trying to carry their groceries, I would ask, "Would you like me to help you with your groceries?" some would just look and keep walking. Others would say, "Yes, thank you."

Most of the houses in that area had steps leading up the front door. Some had porches; others just had vestibules. I would take a bag of groceries in each arm, follow them up the steps, and put the bags on the dining room table or on the kitchen table. They would say "thank you" and would give me a nickel or a dime.

As time went bz and the days passed, Mr. Greenberg came out of his store and asked, "Wesley, would you like to come inside and sweep up for in between customers? I will pay you twenty-five cents at the end of the day." I jumped at the chance. Well, my plan was working. I found a large bottle with a screw-on cap and started to put my quarters and my tips in the bottle when I got home from work. Eventually, I started doing things that I was not expected to do, like when Mrs. Greenburg, who was a short lady, could not reach the upper shelves, I would ask her to let me do it. Eventually, I started to dump potatoes into their bin (and also onions and green beans) and carefully stacking tomatoes and still carrying groceries. Mom say my jar bank and said, "As long as you have a money-making business, you should be giving ten percent to the Lord."

I did not say anything, but I thought, Why? *He isnt helping me.*

Well, summer was coming to an end, and I knew the colder weather and snow was going to hurt my business. So I asked Dad to open a bank account for me. He did, and I had my own bank account of seven dollars,(according to the Holy Bible, it is "the number of completion"). Now Mom would give me an offering envelope with two compartments in it. One side held a nickel, and the other side had two cents. Even though though my Mom brought me to church and even though was out for summer vacation, the sisters liked to have the boys sit on the left-handed side of the church annd the girls on the right-hand side.

On Sundays when Mom did not go to church with me, I would go into the confectionary store at the corner and buy a Coca-Cola for a nickel and two cents worth of Candy. Then I would bypass the church and go to the open field behind the church, find a shady spot, sit down, drink my coke and eat my candy, wait till church let out, and then go home. Stealing from God in any manner is a sin. Thank God for the gift of redemption and the blood of Jusus!

Time moved on. Summer was over, and school opened again in September. This would be a year I would never forget! There were twenty-five children in this class. I had fallen down the cellarsteps and broken my left ankle, so I was walking with crutches. I was told by the principal to go into the classroom early and be seated by the time the rest of the class came in. they started to come in with the class teacher telling them where to sit. When the girls were coming in, I noticed three girls that were together. The second one through the door caught my attention. My heart jumped inside me, and I just wanted to run over and hug her and offer her the seat next to me. After everyone was in class, the bell rang, and we all stood, repeated the Pledge of Allegiance, repeated the Lord's Prayer, and then were told to be seated. The sister in charge sat behind her desk and said, "I think it would be nice if we all introduced ourselves. Let's start on the left front row and go down the first row, then the second, then the last row." So we started standing, telling our names, then sitting down. When it came to those three girls, my ears went up.

The first one stood. "My name is Dolores."

The second girl stood and said, "My name is Nina." My heart pumped like a train going uphill.

The third girl stood and said, "My name is Janett."

Now I knew without even thinking that I had written the name Nina on the inside cover of my loose-leaf book. After every kid had said their name, the sister stood up and said, "My name is Sister Mary Isabell. Now let's begin our studies."

Recess bell rang, and everyone in the classroom went outside except me. Sister Isabell said it would be better for me to stay at my desk because of my ankle. Well, I was eleven years old, taller than anyone in the class, and I could not go outside. I sat at my desk and pouted. Now the people who know me today did not know me then, so they would probably disagree with the next couple of statements. I was very self-conscious about my age, my height, and the fact that I was going through the fourth grade twice. I did not like to stand up at my desk or in front of the classroom and answer any questions or spell any words. I was very shy and backward.

After school had been in session for about a month, Dolores came up to me and asked, "How would you like to attend a pound party?"

I replied, "What is a pound party?"

Then Dolores said, "It's a party where everyone who comes brings a pound of something."

I said, "Yes, but what should I bring, and where is it going to be held?"

Dolores thought and said, "Well, we never seem to have enough bread or rolls, and it is going to be hels at my cousin Janett's house."

Well, I had found out the girls were cousins and that they liked to party. But I said, "I don't know where your cousin lives."

Dolores said, "It's not too far from here. Maybe you could walk us home, and we can show you where she lives."

Wow! I thought. *How lucky can I be to have a date to walk three of the prettiest girls in the class home at the same time?* So after school I met them at the corner of the school yard, and we started off together. My broken ankle had healed, and I didn't have to use the crutches anymore. We walked down Gorsuch Avenue for five blocks.

Then Dolores said, "That's where I live." I made a mental note of 1550 Gorsuch Avenue.

Then Nina said, "And this is where I live." My heart skipped two beats. It was right next door to Dolores's house, 1548 Gorsuch Avenue. In front of Nina's house was a big oak tree (more about that later).

The Janette said, "I live a few blocks from here," and we started to walk to her house. To this day I cannot remember the number or the street that Janette lived on.

So everything was in place for Friday night, starting at six o'clock. For my first pound party, I was excited. The rest of the school week went very slowly. When Friday finally came, I did not think school was going to end. The day finally ended. I had gotten some money to pay for the bead and one dozen rolls. When I got ready to leave, my dad asked, "Where do you think you are going?"

I said, "To a pound party."

He said, "What is a pound party? And a pound of what are you going to get?"

At this point, Grandmother said to Dad, "Oh, Sam, let the boy go and have some fun. He has been working hard on his schoolword all week, and he deserves a little fun."

"Ok," said Dad. "But remember to be home by curfew, which is 9:30."

"OK," I replied, and out the door I ran, down the steps, down Homestead Street. I turned left, still running full speed ahead, onto Locia Raven Road, turned right at Gorsuch Avenue, and slowed to a walk after two blocks. I got to Dolores's house, rapped on the outside door, and waited.

A man came to the door and in a very rough voice asked, "What do you want?"

I asked if Dolores was homek. He said, "Wait here."

He went back inside, and a few minutes later Dolores came to the door. I said, "Hi, are you ready to go to the party?"

She replied, "My dad doesn't let me go to parties alone, so I can't go. But Nina is ready to go. I'll call her and tell her you're waiting for her on the front porch. Have fun."

So I waited and went over the railing to the house next door. I was disappointed because Dolores could not go but bubbling with excitement because I would be walking with Nina for the next five blocks.

She came to the door and said, "Ok, I'm ready. Let's go." She was carrying a large grocery bag, and I asked her if I could carry it for her. She said "OK" and handed me the bag. I was so happy. Here I was walking along with the most beautiful girl in the whole class. As we walked, I brushed my hand?" I could not answer. My tongue was stuck to the roof of my mouth, and I was shaking all over.

We got to Jannett's house too quick, as far as I was concerned. We went up the steps to the porch. Nina opened the door to what I found out later was a vestibule. We went inside, and she rapped on the front door. Jannette came to the door, greeted both of us, and told us to come in. there were a total of twelve people at the party-six girls and six boys. Everyone had a Coke or ginger ale to drink. The girls all helped to make some sandwiches on bread and rolls. There was a cake that got cut, and everyone got a piece. After more Coke and ginger ale, the girls cleaned off the table.

Then someone said, "Let's play a game." *What game can twelve boys and girls play?* I thought. Well, I found out pretty quick. The boys were all given even numbers in secret, and the girls were all given odd numbers in secret. Now because Jannett was the hostess, she said, "I'll go first and start." She went to the front door and opened it and stepped into the vestibule. One of the boys said he would be the postmaster. She whispered to him a number. The postmaster then called an even number, and the boy that had that number went into the vestibule with Jannette. A few minutes later, she came out. She was then the postmaster because the boy inside the vestibule had told her the number he wanted called. So it went like that until Nina's number was called. Then she went in. A few minutes later, the boy came out and called an even number. Now as I said, there were twelve people at the party, and in the game of post office, every other time an odd number is called, a girl goes in, and every time an even number is called, a boy goes in. now there was another boy who was at the party named John. We all called him by his nickname, which was Jeep because he was so fast. When his number got called, he went in and called Nina's number. John came out, and Nina called John's number. This went on four or five times, and then Jannette called an end to the game.

Then Jannette started another game where everybody sat on the floor in a circle-boy, girl, boy, girl-until the circle was complete. Then a quart milk bottle was placed in the center of the circle and was spun, and whoever the top of the bottle pointed to had to kiss the one who had spun the bottle. Jannette's parents came into the room and said, "Ok, kids, it's 9:30, time to go home." I was so mad. I think I was the first one out of the door. Here it was, nine thirty at night—dad said that was my curfew. I had broken curfew, lost my girlfriend, borrowed money from Grandmother, and would probably be punished for being late. *No fair,* I thought. *No fair. Life should not be like this. No fair!* By the time I got home, dad had gone to bed. Grandmother was lying on the couch in the dining room, waiting for me to get home. I asked her if Dad was mad when he went to bed, and before I knew it, a voice from behind me said, "Why don't you ask him yourself?" I explained to Dad what had happened. He replied, "No excuses. We'll deal with this tomorrow when I get home from work."

The next day being Saturday, it was a very long day. Dad was only scheduled to work till noon, but he called Grandmother and said he was going to be working till three o'clock. That was OK with me. When he got home, he was really tired. He said so. Then he said, "I am really too tired to discuss last night and to try to come up with a punishment that fits the crime. So let's just let it go, and you promise not to do it again." I agreed willingly.

At school on Monday, I tried to talk to Nina, but she was busy walking and talking and holding hands with Jeep. I was boiling mad. School let out, and on the way home, I stopped to talk to some of the guys that were standing by the side of the confectionary store. Four of them had started to smoke, like it made them feel big. They tried to get me to try one, I refused. That night when Dad came in from work, I was lying on the floor in front of the radio, waiting for supper to be ready, when Dad walked by me. He stopped, turned toward me, and asked me a question that really caught me by surprise. "Have you been smoking?" he asked.

"No, sir," I replied.

"How come you smell like a chimney?" he said. I told him about the guys on the corner that were smoking. He looked at me and didn't say anything, but he looked like he did not believe me. He said, "If you want to start smoking, it's OK with me. But if you do, you smoke a pipe or a cigar. No cigarettes. If I catch you with a pack of cigarettes in this house and the is oper, I will make you eat every one of them. Is that clear? Do you understand?"

I replied, "Yes, sir."

The next day after school, when I got to the house, my uncle Jack was sitting on the front porch steps, waiting for his friends to pick him up in their car. I asked him, "How come Dad thought I was smoking cigarettes? How could he know?"

Jack said, "He could smell it on your clothes. If you are going to smoke cigarettes, when you come into the house, go upstairs, take off your clothes and underwear, take a shower, brush your teeth, and make sure you use plenty of mouthwash. Then take your clothes and underwear down to the cellar, put soap and hot water in the washtubs, and let them sit there overnight. That will kill the smoke smell."

A few weeks went by, and one afternoon, I followed Nina, Dolores, and Jannette on their way home. They saw and asked why I was following them. I said, "I have a problem with two math questions and wanted to see if Dolores could help me with them." They accepted my reason, and I got to walk with them. After Dolores had helped me with the problem, I got ready to leave, and Nina was standing on her front porch. She said to me, "I am sorry for hurting you the way I did. Will you please forgive me? And can we be boyfriend and girlfriend?"

I was delighted. I asked her if she meant it, and what about Jeep? She said he had another girlfriend and that they were through. I was so happy I took out my pocketknife, and on the big oak tree that stood in front of her house, I carved a heart with the inscription that said "Wes love Nina." Happiness filled my soul. We kissed, and I went home.

Now it was getting close for school to start, and Nina said, "We, my family and all, are going to my uncle's house. It is on the waterfront. Would you like to go with me?" of course, I said yes.

So the week went by. I was supposed to be at Nina's house by 6:30 a.m. I was there by 6:00 a.m. Everyone started to bring things out of the house and then pack them in the trunk. We started getting into the car. First the driver, then someone I did not know (a girl) sat next to the driver. Then someone else I did not know filled in the front seat. Then Jannette got in. Her boyfriend sat in the middle of the seat, and she sat on his lap. Then one of the boys from class sat behind the driver, and another girl from class sat on his lap. Nina told me to get in and sit behind the passenger seat. I did. Nina got in and sat on my lap. Oh, I was in heaven. She closed the door, and we were off and running. Everyone was talking and laughing. It was starting off as a beautiful day. It took about forty-five minutes to get to the shore house. We parked, unload the car, took everything out of the trunk, and just about that time, another car pulled up. And who was the first one out of the car? That's right. It was Jeep. He talked to Nina, they went off somewhere, and for the rest of the day I was alone. Nina came back a couple of times, but then it was time to leave. We loaded back in the car that we came down. I was happy to have Nina back on my lap, and I put my arms around her and had a joyful ride home.

CHAPTER 6

School was getting ready to start. By this time, I was going into the sixth grade. I was still the tallest and oldest kid in class. One of the boys that was in class had a paper route. His family was getting ready to move, and he asked me if I would like to take his place. Of course, I said yes. He made the necessary call to his distributor, and I went round with him to find out where the paper route was. When I met the distributor, he was surprisedthati had learned the route. He told me I had the job. I had to deliver fifty papers, Monday through Saturday, and if there was a "stop paper" notice on any of the papers, I was to go to the house, try to collect what was owed, and get a restart notice. The route manager would meet me somewhere on the route on Friday afternoon, collect any money I had collected, and pay me my two dollars for deliveries. Now that I had a job, I didn't have much time to hang with the gang.

One day, after serving my papers, I was walking home. I saw a big moving van taking furniture into a house on the corner of Homestead Street and Independence Street. I didn't think any more about it. The school year ended, and summer vacation arrived. I learned that serving papers in the summer is a lot harder than serving in the winter. One day, when I had finished the paper route, I had gone home, had dinner, and was walking up the street. I saw two girls coming towards me. One was my sister, Loretta, and I did not know the other girl.

Loretta said, "Hey, Wes, this is my new friend Pat. She and her family just moved into the house on the corner."

I said hi. She said, "Hi, my older sister wants meet you."

I said that we sometimes played catch footballin the street in front of their house. "I may see her there," I said, and then I continued on around the corner to the confectionary store. A few days later, on a Saturday, I had finished serving papers and finished eating. I walked up the street. Some of the guys already had the football out and were tossing it around, when someone said, "Hey, let's play touch." So we chose sides, but we had an uneven number (can you guess what it was? Right, seven-the number of completion).

Just before we started to play, a voice called from the side, "Hey, can I play?" All the guys looked and then looked at each other and said, "That's a girl!" We were playing two-hand touch. We all looked at each other and then looked back at the girl. One of the fellows yelled to her, "Wait a minute." We all got in a huddle. Some of the guys said right away to let her play.

I glanced over to the steps where she was sitting and said to the guys, "You all see the man who is sitting there with her? I assume that's her father. If she plays and one of us touches her in an inappropriate place and he comes after us, who's going to take him on, and who's going to run?"

we took a vote. She won by a four-to-three vote. She came off the steps and got in the huddle with the rest of her team. I was on the other team. A couple of downs went by, and she was on the line. I was playing full back for the team that I was on. They snapped the ball. She was running down the sideline. The quarterback threw the ball to her. She caught it. Took three steps, and ran right into me. I pushed her with both hands right into a hedge fence that was on the far side of the street. I told her I was sorry buyt that was the way we played touch football-hard and fast.

She said, "Shut up and help me out here."

I asked her, "What's your name?"

She replied, "Colleen." Now at that time, the name didn't mean anything to me.

Time went by. School was still in session, and a lot of the guys that used to hang up around the confectionary store were now gathering on Colleens's front porch. I quit my paper route and answered an ad in the paper for an uscher at the Boulevard Theater. The applicant had to be at least sixteen years of age. Now I was only fourteen. Could I do it? I did it. I applied, got the job, and started to work two days later.

Now it was almost time for school to dismiss for summer, and I was really looking forward to vacation. Mom got a call from the principal at school and found out that I was in danger of failing, and if I did fail, would she want to enroll me in summer school? When Mom told me about the phone call, I asked her not to sign me up for summer school, assuring her that I would really buckle down and work hard to pass. I worked hard by paying attention in school, doing my assigned homework in the afternoon, after school, and then going to work at the Boulevard Theater on Greenmount Avenue at night. Well, the final week of school that year came, and Sister Isabell had given us some homework with long division problems that she thought might be on next week's final tests. The next day she reviewed the questions, and when she came to one particular question on long division, she said that there was only one person in the whole class that got the right answer. She wrote the question on the blackboard and turned toward the class. With a smile on her face, she said, "Wesley, will you please come to the blackboard and show the class how you got the answer?" I was totally surprised. I rose to my feet, shaking like a leaf in a windstorm, got to the blackboard, took the chalk from the teacher's hand, and started to solve the problem. When I put down the right answer, everyone in the classroom started to clap, including the teacher. "See what you can accomplish if you put your mind to it?" she said.

The final day of school came. We all cleaned out our desks, and when the bell rang, we all left. We all stood around in the playground saying so long to some who were leaving for the whole summer and to some who were going to be moving. We would probably never see them again. That night I went to work at the Boulevard, and it was marquee night. One of the other usher and I were told to change the marquee. Now what we had to do was after the last show had started, the assistant manager would give us a piece of paper. Written on the paper was the name of the next movie that was going to be shown there for the next two to three days. It also had the names of the male and female who starred in the picture. The two of us had to get the eleven-foot ladder from behind the movie screen, carry it out the back door and around to the front of the movie theater, and then put the ladder up. Then we would flip a coin to see who was going to climb up the ladder and remove the letters that were there and drop them one at a time to the one who stayed on the ground. The one who stayed on the ground had to arrange the letters on the ground in order to spell out the name of the actor and actress who starred in the picture and, on the next line, the name of the movie that was coming. Because most movies played at the Boulevard three or four days, we only had to change the marquee twice a week. I was new, but it didn't take long for me to find out that you don't touch the neon lights. Because when you do, you get an electric shock that can knock you off that ladder. By the way, the guy who was on the ground had to toss the letters up to the guys who was at the top of the ladder. He hadto catch them, and if he missed, when the letters hit the sidewalk, they would usually break.

School was out now, and I didn't see too much of Nina. One day I was talking with Colleen and some of the guys on her front porch when Nina came walking down Independence Street. As she walked by, she started to do some somersaults, and as she had on a dress, it went up when she went over. I made a smart remark. She waved her hand and kept going. I went down to see her the next day after school because she had avoided contact with me all day at school. She came to the door and greeted me with, "what do you want?"

"Just to talk to you annd tell you how sorry I am about the smart remark I made yesterday."

"Oh," she replied, "is your other girlfriend mad at you too? Well, that's tough. I don't ever want to see you again!" And she went back into her house.

So I left and walked back home very depressed. The girl I fell in love with four years ago in the fourth grade never wanted to see me again.

The school year was almost over, and I know it was going to be a long summer. I went to work at the Boulevard that evening, and when the show was over, I walked down Greenmount Avenue to a little tavern hamburger shop. Hamburgers were ten cents each, and Cokes were five cents each plus two cents deposit on each bottle that you got back when you brought the bottles back. I walked down Homestead Street to Colleen's house. She was sitting on her front steps. I saw her, and I asked if she would like a hamburger and a Coke. She said, "Sure." We sat there and ate the hamburgers and drank the Cokes.

The next day at school I was really tired. The time I spent with Colleen did not end till after 1:00 a.m. One of my friends who also hung around on Colleen's front porch got hold of me and said, "Colleen asked me if there was something wrong with her because you have not tried to kiss her." I thaned him for telling me.

Two weeks later, my family had a big party at the house, and it was full of people. Later that night I tried to sneak out the front door. Mom caught me and asked, "Where do you think you are going?"

"Just going to run around the block for good luck," I replied.

"OK."

And off I went. Now when I got up to Colleen's house, she was standing at the basement side door of her house. I rushed up to her house, took her in my arms, and kissed her on her lips for at least five minutes. Then I ran down the alley to my house, just in case Mom might be standing on the porch to see what direction I came from. Some time later I asked her what she thought of the first time I kissed her. She said she closed her eyes, and she heard church bells, horns blowing, and fireworks going off. I had to remind her that the first time I kissed her, it was on New Year's Eve.

CHAPTER 7

Now a coupple of weeks went by, and after school was over, I was walking Colleen home from school and carrying her books and mine. You see, I used to leave home for school in the morning and go to Colleen's house to pick her up and carry her books to school for her. You see, she did not go to the same school I did. She went to Clifton Park Junior High School that was on Harford Road, seven blocks down Homestead Street or down Gorsuch Avenue. I would drop her off at school in the morning and pick her up in the afternoon and walk her home, not every day but sometimes. I knew if my schoolwork started to fail, the sister would call my mom and I would be grounded.

One day Colleen told me her mother was going to have a baby and that the excitement of city living was to strenuous for her. The doctor had recommended moving to the suburbs. A couple of weeks later, I saw a moving truck at her house. I met her that afternoon and asked if she was just going to move without letting me know. She said yes. It was just too hard to say goodbye because the really loved me. Well, when I heard that, I made up my mind that no matter where she moved to, I would find her. The move truck was loaded, and her mom and dad came out to the car followed by Colleen's sisters-Pat, Fran, Fay, and a very small sister named Kitty. They started to get into the car. She hugged me and said she loved me. She kissed me with teardrops running down her face (I was crying too).

"Where are you moving to?" I asked.

She said, "It's some place called Woodlawn." She told me later that when they had driven away and she had finally stopped crying, her mother had said, "Well, you will probably never see that boy again."

Meanwhile school had ended. Marks were in, and I had failed seventh grade. The sister recommended summer school to my mother. Mom asked me if I wanted to go to summer school. I replied, "If I didn't learn in ten months of regular school, how do you expect me to learn in three months of summer school?" Well, she did not insist. One thing I forgot to mention earlier was that while school was out on Saturdays and on holidays, Colleen's father was a route supervisor for Cloverland Milk Co. He was in charge of five routes. He had to ride with the route salesman one week before they went on vacation, and the week they were off, he would run their route. I asked him if he needed any help. I would be glad to help him. He took me up on my offer, and after they had moved, I asked him, "How can I get to Woodlawn from here?"

He explained, "Well, seeing as you don't have a driver's license or a car, your best bet would be by streetcar and bus." He said, "Take the number 17 streetcar to Greenmount Avenue. Transfer to the number 8 streetcar, and ask the driver to let you off at the number 26 bus stop. Take the bus to the end of the line. Transfer to the number 32 streetcar to the end of the line, and that is Woodlawn. But after you get to Woodlawn, you have another five miles to go on Windsor Mill Road on the even hours and back on the odd hours." So there it was, all laid out for me.

Well, I quit my job at the movie theater. I got a daytime job at Zips Photo Supply Co. They had an ad in the *Baltimore Paper*. I answered it and got the job. The job was to be a film cutter. The customer would bring in their film from their cameras. The cleric at the counter would put it in an envelope with the customer's name on it. The envelope would go into the development room where it was taken out of its package, opened up, and hung on a long hanger opened, with the envelope number on the long hanger. The film would go into the developing tank. After they were developed, they were moved to a room with fans that would blow them dry. After they were dried, they were taken to where I was sitting. In front of me was a table that could be adjusted to cut the negative to the proper size. The scissors were worked by your foot. You did not want your feet to cut faster than your hands could feed the negative. I only worked from nine to six, with an hour off for lunch. Grandmother usually packed me two sandwiches for lunch and a piece of a cake or pie that she had bake, but usually there was none left. Out behind the photo shop was a small fenced-in yard that could only be entered through the shop. My salary was fifty cents an hour with Saturday, Sunday, and holidays off (no pay for holidays).

After a month I noticed that I did not need a whole hour for lunch. So I got a small folding table and a chair, put them in the backyard, and during lunchtime after I had finished eating, I started to build plastic airplanes that I could buy at the five and ten cent store on Greenmount Avenue.

I got a little bit of money saved up and got ready to start going to Woodlawn, I followed the directions Colleen's father gave me, and in about one and one-half hours, I arrived in Woodlawn. I waited for the Windsor Mill Road bus. I got on board, dropped my dime in the box, and the told the driver where I wanted to go. He said he knew what house the lived in, and when I got off the bus, I could see why. It was a big two-story house with an attique. It had a driveway on the right side of the house and a garage ar the rear of the house. I walked up the steps and rapped on the door. Colleen's father answered the door and said Colleen had gone to the store up the road to get him a pack of cigarettes.

"She should be back soon," he said. "Sit down and wait."

So I did, and he and I talked about everything was going and how I was maiking out. A good half hour went by, and Colleen had not returned. I was getting worried, and her father was getting mad. I wanted to spend time with her; he wanted to smoke. Finally, Colleen came in, handed her father his cigarettes, and said, "Sorry it took so long, but while I was walking up to the store for your cigarettes, one of the pilots from the airport asked if I would like to fly up to washington in his open cockpit airplane."

"You know I just could not resist," she said.

Her dad said, "It's OK with me, but what about Wes?" He pointed over to me.

She turned and said, "Oh, I didn't see you sitting there. How are you?"

I was totally unprepared for this kind of hello. Her father said, "Maybe you two should go for a walk." We did. We went outside, around the side of the house, and then she turned and put her arms around me and kissed me. "I'm glad you're here," she said. We kissed again. Then I heard a loud noise like an airplane. I looked, and just outside of the back yard of the house. Now I was upset.

I said, "How long have these little airplane trips been going on?"

She replied that that was only the second time. The first time another pilot took her it was on a double cockpit plane, and it was oper. He showed her what dfun it was to do barrel rolls, loop-de-loop, fly upside down, buss the field. "Oh, it was so much fun," she said.

Then I asked her, "And just what do they expect in return.?"

She said, "Nothing. They just like me."

"Well," I said, "Nobody does nothing for nothing. Just watch your step." That was the beginning of our first fight. The bus was coming down the street. I hailed the driver, got on the bus, and headed for home.

Sometime had gone before I cooled off enough to call Colleen on the phone. She answered, and I asked how she was doing. She said, "OK," and we talked for a little while and then hung up. I had quit my full-time job at the photo shop and was working with her father. He had put in a good word for me, and I got hired for inside the plant as a bottle washer. Things were going along fine. I had gotten back together with Colleen.

One day my mother called me into the dining room and asked me a question. She said, "Just what do you intend to do with your life?"

I replied, "I really don't know. Probably get married, have children, get a car. Get a home. I really hadn't planned that far ahead."

She said, "I always thought that you would become a priest."

I said, "No, Mom. Priests don't get married."

She replied, "Well, if you think that you are going to marry that girl that lived up the street, I will be over my dead body." Four weeks later my mother went into Union Memorial Hospital. She never came home again.

That night I was out at Colleen's house when my father called. He was angry and upset. Over the phone he said, "Your mother is dead. You'd better get your ass home here!" Then slammed down the phone. I hung up the receiver and, with tears running down my face, said to Colleen, "My mother is dead."

Her father said, "I'll get the car and take you home."

"I rode my bike out here. It's outside. I have to take it home."

"I'll put it in the trunk. You can't ride a bike in your condition." He put the bike in the trunk and drove me home. Colleen sat between her dad and me. When we got to the house, her father turned the car off, went to the trunk, and took out my bike. Colleen got out so I could get out, gave me a big hug and kiss, and said "I'm sorry about your mother. Remember, I love you."

I went into the house. Grandmother was sitting in the dinning room, crying. I asked, "Where is Dad?"

She replied, "He and your sister went to the undertakers to make arrangements for your mother's funeral."

When they got home, Dad took one look at me and, in a very "you're not worth it" wave, said nothing and went to bed. I went to work the next morning and told my boss what happened. He offered his apology and said, "You have three days funeral leave coming to you. Take today and the next three days off." Later I found out from my sister that Dad blamed me for Mom's death. Colleen came to Mom's viewing one night, and when we walked up to the side of the casket, she started crying very hard, turned, and ran outside. I ran after her, and she told me that my mother lying in the coffin had said to her, "I don't like you!"

Well, life such as it was, went on. Pat, Colleen's youngster sister, met a boy named Paul. Now Paul had a motorbike and used to ride it to see Pat. Sometimes he would take Colleen for a ride too. He met a guy who lived in Woodlawn, not too far from where the girls lived. I don't know who suggested it, but a couple of times when Paul showed up to take Pat bike riding, the guy would show up to take Colleen riding with them. Perfectly innocent? Yeah right! He was a kind of short guy. When he went to kiss Colleen once, he had to stand on the first step to be able to kiss her.

One evening when I went out to spend some time with my girl, she was out bike riding with him. I saw red! If I have any Irish blood in me, it was at the boiling point! He drove up in the front of the house. Colleen got off, came over to me, kissed me on the cheek, and said hi. I just looked at her and said nothing. The other boy had gotten off his motorcycle, turned off the engine, and walked over to where Colleen and I were. He said hi and told me his name, then stuck out his hand like he wanted to shake. I shove his hand away, grabbed him by his shirt, pulled him up to me, and told him, "If I ever come here again and find out that you have taken her for a ride on your motorcycle, kissed her, or in any other way touched her, I am going to grind you right into the dirt that you're standing on."

I carried him over to the second step of the house and stood him on it. "If you have the guts, swing, and make the first one good because you won't get a second one." Colleen was holding me back. I must have been screaming pretty loud because she came out of the house and grabbed me.

Colleen said to the boy, "You had better go. I think he is mad." The boy got on his motorcycle and left.

Now after things had settled down, Pat and Paul went inside the house. Colleen's father went into the house after he had a long talk with me. Colleen had gone on into the house earlier. I sat on the glider, swinging back and forth and hoping that boy would come back. I had calmed down and was thinking about what I had come all this distance to ask Colleen. She came out, sat down on the glider, and said, "I'm sorry. I didn't think you would get so upset."

I told her, "I came all the way out here tonight to ask you a very important question. And what do I find? You sitting here waiting for me? No, you were out riding on a motorcycle with another man and you had your arms around his waist. Then instead of him doing the right thing and driving away, he comes up to me like we were going to be best friends. Do you think I have Any right to be mad?"

"Don't answer," I said. "I'm going to ask you the question that I wanted to ask you for a long time. Will you marry me? Just answer yes or no."

She looked at me with tears in her eyes and smiled and said, "Yes, I would love to marry you." We held each other, kissed several times, and the bus that was supposed to pick me up went right by. I didn't have enough money to call for a cab. I didn't want to ask her dad because I wanted her to tell her family after I left. I reached into my pocket, took out the engagement ring that I had bought, and put it on her finger. We kissed again.

I said, "Now remember, you are engaged to me. No more flying with other men, no more bike riding with other men. It's you and me together, always."

Paul came out on the porch and said, "Wes, you missed the bus. How are you going to get down to the streetcar line?"

I replied, "I don't know. Walk I guess."

He said, "I've got my motorbike. I'll be glad to give you a ride on the back."

I said, "Thanks, I would appreciate it."

He got on his motorbike and started it up. I kissed Colleen, got on the back, and we started off down the long dark road. Now going down Windsor Mill Road, just before you get to Woodlawn, there is a steep hill. Just before we got to the top of the hill, Paul hollered back, "As soon as we start down the hill, put your feet down and drag them. I don't any brakes!" Now I had learned from scouting that discretion is the better part of valor. I put both feet down firmly, stood up, and was perfectly safe walking down the hill.

When I got home, I called Colleen. "did you tell your family?" I asked. "What did they say?"

She replied, "They were extremely happy and wanted to know what date we had set so they can make plans."

"What date did give you them?" I asked.

She said, "I told them I had to talk to you first because we did not set a date or a time. But I was thinking about September. Would that be OK with you?"

I told her September would be fine and the next time I came to see her we would set the date and time. She called me back the next day and said, "Pat and Paul are going to get married also, and Pat and I had thought about having a double wedding. How does that sound to you?"

I said, "Great. It's OK with me."

So the weekend came, and I was on my way to Woodlawn again. When I got there, Paul had not yet arrived. We waited for him to get there so we could se the exact date and time. Paul finally came, and we voted on a date that all four of us approved. So the date we set was July 23, 1949. Colleen and her sister, Pat, went to the courthouse in Ellicott City to get the marriage licenses. The girls made all the arrangements. I had to try to get time off from the dairy. My boss said something big was in the works and that he really didn't want me to take time off. A few days later, he came to me and said, "The best I can do is give you days off on Friday, Saturday, and Sunday."

"Great," I said.

Now I had not told my father about my plans because I knew he would explode! So I waited till the very last minute to tell him. He screamed and hollered at the of his voice. He screamed, "If you go through with this plan of yours, don't ever come back into this house again!"

My grandmother came into the room and yelled at my father, "You listen here, Sam, that boy is my grandson, and he has much right to come into this house as you do. He and his wife will be welcomed!"

Time went by, and we finally got everything ready for the wedding. Now we found out that because Colleen was eighteen, she did not need her parents to sign the weeding license application. But they had to sign for Pat because she was only sixteen. I was only seventeen, but a friend of mine signed for me. Well, everything was set for the wedding. I took a change of clothes to Colleen's house the day before the wedding and spent that night after work sleeping on the couch in the living room.

Now after work, her father and I drove home together. We were both excited. The wedding was scheduled for 8:00 p.m. Colleen's family all drove up in the family car. Paul and I rode up with the best man and his wife. The best man stood for both of us, and his wife was the maid of honor for both girls. Her mother sat on the first row of seats, and Paul's mom and dad set on the second row of seats. The organ played "Here Comes the Bride." Paul and I stood at the front with the best man standing between us. Down the aisle came his wife, the maid of honor, and a few feet behind her came the two girls and their father. He had one girl on each arm, and the look of pride and happiness on his face was something to see.

The service ended, and we all got back in the cars and headed back to house for refreshments. We had made arrangements to spend two nights and two days in Washington, DC. Now I was seventeen years old. I had been going out with Colleen since I was fourteen. Eating and the bus ride to Washington were not exactly what was on my mind (think about it). We finally got to the hotel in Washington, got our key registered, and got into our room. I started to undress, but before I had gone too far, Colleen went into the bathroom an locked the door. "What are you doing?" I yelled.

She replied, "I'm going to take a shower."

I almost wanted to tear that door off the hinges. Instead, I started to unpack the suitcase and hag up the clothes. After about twenty to twenty-fives minutes, a scream came from the inside the bathroom. I rushed to the door and tried to force the door open, but it did not budge. "What's wrong? Are you all right?" I hollered.

She replied through the door, "I'm OK."

I asked why she had screamed.

"Nothing's wrong. I'll tell you later."

About ten minutes later, she unlocked the door and came out wearing her nightgown. I said, "Why do you have that on?"

She said, "You are going to have wait another week. It is my time of the month." I was totally unprepared for this event. I spent the night sleeping with my wife. The next morning at breakfast, I told Pat and Paul that Colleen and I were leaving of the first bus going back to Baltimore. They stayed and had a good time. We left and came home. Monday, when I went to work, people asked me how it felt to be a newly married mad. Without going into lengthy explanation, I just said, "Same as before I was married."

Well, things went along like normal and about two weeks later, the big surprise that was coming got here. The management announced that they were closing the home delivery section of the dairy. Here I was, a newly married man, and now I would have no job and no income. The weeks went by, and my father-in-law said to me, "How would you like to learn how to lay bricks?" He said that he was a bricklayer by trade and that he could teach me how to lay brick and make a better paycheck. The following week. We spent the first three days going from job to job, but nobody wanted to hire me. Colleen's father said I should call him Pop, so I did. Pop and I went to a job site that had to have seven houses built by the end of the week. Otz, as every one called him, was the man in charge and he was desperate to get good bricklayers. He hired Pop and me.

We finished the job on time. Pop saw on the next job we went to that I was having trouble bending my wrist the right way with the trowel. So after work he unlocked the trunk and turned and said to me, "Pick out fifteen bricks, take some of the mud (mortar) that was left over, and put it on one of the boards in the trunk." He wanted me to practice. He told me how to move my wrist and spread the mortar, put down four bricks, spread the mud out, built four more bricks on top of the other bricks, put them in the trunk, and then take them back to the job site. He tried, I tried, but nothing worked.

After three weeks, on payday, Otz, the boss, held out my pay envelope in front of everyone on the job site and shouted as loud as he could, "Hey, Watts, if you want your paycheck this week, you'd better back up to get it."

I walked up to him face-to-face. Then I added, "And just to get one up on you, I quit!" And with that I walked of the job site and waited for Pop to finish up for the day.

When Pop got to the car, I thought I was going to get a lecture. He just looked at me and said, "If you hadn't told him off, I was going to. Now what are you going to do?"

"I don't know. Wait till Monday and start looking around to find a job I can do?" (Now do you remember in chapter 2 when I said I heard one word-*wait*? What was going to happen? Was that what the word meant?)

Pop said to me, "Do you know anything about working in gas stations?"

I said, "NO, but I can learn."

Pop drove toward home. we got to the end of Gwynn Oak Avenue, turned right onto the Windsor Mill Road, went to the top of the hill, and pulled into the gas station with the big red, white, and blue sign with one word written on it-*American*. A man came out of the office. He walked with a limp, and he carried his right arm in front of him bent at the elbow. Pop talked to him for a few minutes, then beckoned for me to come over. When I walked over, Pop said, "Wes, this is Mr. Pearpont. He owns this gas station, and he needs someone to help him."

Mr. Pearpont said, "do you know anything about gas stations?"

I said, "No, sir, but I can learn."

He said, "Well, it's a lot more to it than just pumping gas. If you're willing to learn, I'm willing to teach you, what do you say?"

I said, "How much will I make?"

He laughed, "I'll pay you fifty cents an hour to start. As soon as you learn how to check oil, put air in tires, and clean windshields, I'll raise your pay to seventy-five cents per hour. If you learn how to fix flats and rotate tires, I'll raise your pay to one dollar an hour, and you get to keep whatever anybody gives you as a tip."

We shook hands, and he said, "Be here tomorrow at nine o'clock, and we'll get you started."

I was so happy. Pop drove the other mile and a half and pulled into the driveway. I could not wait. I jumped out of the car, ran up the steps, and busted in through the front door. Colleen was helping her mother fix dinner. "I got a new job. I start tomorrow, and it's only down the road!" Pop came in, and while we were eating dinner, Pop told them all about the events of the day.

Colleen finally said, "Well, that's good news about the job just down the road, but you had better work hard and get that one dollar an hour. I'm pregnant!"

I almost fell off the chair. I was going to be a father! We had waited to have a baby till some time went by after we were married because back in those days when a couple got married young, everyone would think it was a shotgun wedding-that the girl had gotten pregnant before the marriage took place. So here we were, getting ready for our firstborn baby. Then the name planning started. "What do you want?" people would ask me. (I found out that when you work in a gas station, everybody knows everybody else's business.) "A boy, naturally," I would reply. Of course, Colleen wanted a girl. So, we started thinking about names. If it was a boy, we could name him Henry (after her father) or Samuel (after my father) or Wesley (after me) or Kenneth (after my best friend).

"If it's a girl, we can name her after you or after your mother, Evelyn, or after my mother, Mildred, or after my grandmother, Catherine." And just to liven things up, I suggested, "We could call her after my first girlfriend, Nina. "That name was ruled out fast.

Colleen said, "Let's name her Gene Marie." I agreed. For some reason or another, I don't know why we stuck with reviewing boys names only. (Was God trying to tell us something?) we waited and waited. Nine months was never going to arrive.

Meanwhile, Phil was working me hard, and I was learning fast. I had found out where to find the gas tanks on some of the newer cars and how to check the oil, water, battery, and transmission fluid on vehicles. I also learned how to replace batteries, repair tires, and replace windshield wipers. Phil was true to his word. The first tires he had me fixing were off big dump trucks with split-rim tire wheels. They were tough. Then I found out that his brother owned the trucking business that hauled dirt and concrete and sand, so he had a lot of business for my boss. True to his word. Phil gave me a raise. Also, when the baby was born, he kicked up another fifty cents in my paycheck.

Well, the time came, and it was time for Colleen to deliver. We took her to the hospital, and they took her into the delivery room. We waited all the afternoon, and finally, the doctor came out and said, "It's a false alarm. She will not be delivering tonight, but you all should go home and try to rest. You can't see her because she is intensive care and cannot have visitors."

So we went home. The next day we called again. No difference. We talked to the doctor, and he said, "It is not unusual for a first-time mother to have these false labor pains. If she is not ready by tomorrow, we will induce labor. Don't worry. We'll take good care of both of them."

The next day was my day off from work. After calling the hospital three times, Pop said, "Let's go to a movie. If nothing has happened yet, it probably won't happen at all today." So he and I went to the movies, and to this day, I could not tell you what picture we saw. When we got home from the movie, I called the hospital and asked if there had been any change in Colleen's condition. The nurse said, "Hold on please," and put me on hold. What seemed like hours and hours went by, and then the doctor came to the phone. My heart jumped into my mouth as I asked the doctor if there had been any change in her condition.

He said, "Oh yes, Mr. Watts, you are the father of a strong and healthy baby boy. Congratulations."

I said, "Can I see her and him?"

The doctor said, "Come on over. I'll make arrangements."

Her dad and I got in the car and drove to the hospital. When we got there, they had put her in a room. When we got to the room and went in, she looked up and said, "I hope you had a good time at the movies because I didn't." I kissed her and held her tight and whispered in her ear, "I love you." Then I asked, "Have you seen the baby?"

She said, "Yes, but only for a few minutes."

I asked the nurse if we could see the baby. She said she would bring him to the room for a few minutes. She brought him, we all fused over him, and then I asked Colleen, "What are we going to call him?"

She said, "You name him."

I said, "Kenneth Wesley."

Colleen said, "that's it." The nurse took him back to his place.

Now when we brought her and the home from the hospital, things got a little hectic. He would cry at night, and Colleen or I would have to hold him or walk around the living room with him. We decided to look for an apartment. We went through the newspaper every evening looking at the houses and apartments for rent. Low and behold, half a mile up the road there was a small dirt road. One-and-one-half miles down the road was a two-story house that had an apartment for rent. We figured out a budget. It was tight, but if everything went just right, we could afford it. But you all know everything doesn't go right all the time. We had to buy paregoric for the baby. But things weren't too bad. I told Phil that I was going to have to quit and gave him two weeks' notice.

He said, "You're a good learner and a good worker. What can I do to change your mind?" I told him with the added expense of the baby and the rent on the apartment, we just could not make it on my salary.

He said, "Sorry, Wes, I just can't pay you any more than what you make now. But if you can't find another job paying more in two weeks, just hang on here till you find something."

CHAPTER 8

A couple of weeks went by, and I saw an ad in the paper that an Atlantic service station needed an experienced service station helper to apply in person at the station on Gwynn Oak Avenue. Apply immediately. The next day I took a day off and walked the half mile from Phil's American station to the streetcar stop at Gwynn Oak Avenue Road. I took the streetcar up to Gwynn Oak Avenue, got off, and there on the right-hand side of the streetcar about halfway down the block was the Atlantic sign. Just across the street from where I got off the streetcar was another service station, and there the sign said "American." Something inside me said, "someday you will work at that station," but I did not listen" and walked down to the Atlantic station.

The owner was sitting in the office, smoking a cigar. He saw me walk in and said, "What can I do for you?"

I didn't like the way he asked, but I was desperate. I said, "I saw your ad in the newspaper for an experienced service station attendant, and I am here to apply for the job."

He looked at me, removed his cigar from his mouth, leaned back in his chair, and said to me, "What makes you think I should hire you?"

I was getting a little more than I wanted, and without thinking, I said, "You need an experienced service station attendant. I have that experience, and I need a job."

He sat up straight in his chair, reached into his desk drawer, pulled out an employment application, and said, "Fill this out. you've got a job."

Shaking like a leaf in a windstorm, I filled out the application. I handed the man the completed application. He looked it over and said, "Who do you think you are kidding? You are only a kid, and you put on your application that you are married and have a child."

I said, "That is correct, sir, and it was not shotgun wedding. We both wanted to get married, so we did."

He said, "Son of a gun! You got the job. When can you start?"

"Tomorrow," I said.

He said, "Be here at seven a.m. ready for work."

I said, "How much does the job pay?"

He said, "Three hundred dollars twice a month."

I thought to myself, *Wow, that's six hundred dollars a month. That ought to keep us healthy.* We shook hands, and I left and went back home. I stopped on the way back and told Phil. He wished me good luck and said he was glad I got a job close to home. And with a smile on his face, he said, "Don't steal any of my customers." We shook hands and said to each other "see ya around."

Well, things were looking up. I went to work the next day in a pair of gray pants and a blue shirt. It was summer time and a hot day. When I got to work, John was already at his desk. "Is that what you intend to work in?" he asked. I said it was all I had to wear because I turned in my Amoco uniform.

"Well," he said, "When the uniform man comes in on Tuesday, give him your sizes for shirts and pants." When the uniform man came in on Tuesday, I gave him my sizes.

He said, "The uniform serves you with four shirts and two pair of pants. In the winter time, we deliver on Tuesday and Friday. You get the same number of shirts and pants, but we also supply you with two jackets. The cost to you is three dollars in the summer and five dollars in the winter." I asked how was I supposed to pay for cleaning and paying. He said John would deduct it out of my paycheck.

Things went OK for the first two weeks except John kept calling me kid. And finally on the third week, I told him, "My name is Wesley, but you can call me Wes. In case you don't know, that's the same amount of letters that are in the name Kid." I only worked there for four months, and then I quit. I found another job on Harford and North Avenue at a place called Bond Bread Bakery. It was delivering bread, pies, and doughnuts and collecting bills at the end of the week. I had to work six days a week but was off on Sundays. I worked there for about two months and decided that was not a job I wanted until I could retire.

One day, as I was working my bread route, I passed by the Amoco station on Gwynn Oak Avenue and stopped in. I talked to the manager and told him I would like to know if he was hiring any help. He told me that station and all other stations wearing the American sign were company-owned stations and that I could fill out an application at another station that was over near Park Circle. I left, and two days later, I stopped at a traffic light at North Avenue and Harford Road. I was delivering to a small grocery store when I saw a sign on the window of a store. "Help wanted: Apply within." I went in and stated that I was interested in employment. They gave me an application to fill out and asked how soon I could fill it out. I told them tomorrow. The man then said, "and when would you able to start?" I said the first of next week. I filled out the application, returned it, and the man said, "Do you have a problem working in cold freezing weather?" I thought that was unusual question to ask when it was June and the weather was in the high eighties. He told me to give my notice and report the first of next week. I gave my notice, and the first day of the following week, I reported to the man. He said, "Come with me." We walked two blocks up the street and saw a two story white building with a sign hanging across the front that said Devile Deal Ice Cream Company. He took me inside and said, "This is Mike. Mike is the plant manager. He will place you where he needs you most. Good luck." We shook hands, and he left. Then I found out why the other man wanted to know why I had any bad feelings about working in the cold.

I was going to be working in the freezer where the ice cream was stored. The room next door to the freezer room was where they put the cream into molds. They put the ice cream on a tray with twelve molds on each tray, put them on a tall rack that had four rows holding two trays on each row, and then they would put the racks filled with trays over to the room where I was working. I was to take this rack filled with trays and put them into the big walk-in freezer for exactly one half hour. Then I was to take that rack to them so they could put the chocolate over the ice cream and shove the rack back to me to put back in the freezer for one hour. Then I would take the rack out to the door on the other side of the room to have all the chocolate-covered ice cream put into packages. When that was done, the ice-cream bars came back to me to store in the freezer till delivery time the next day. I didn't stay at that job too long.

Now while I was changing jobs, our baby boy was growing up. He was now three years old. When I got home from work one night, my wife said, "You got a phone call today from some man that you filled out an application for. He wants you to call him." I dialed the number and was surprised that it was the personal manager from American Oil Co. he asked if I was still interested in training for an assistant manager's job at one of their service stations. I told him yes, I was.

He said, "When can you come to Gwynn Oak Avenue and start training?"

I said, "The first of the week."

He said, "I'll see you there."

I told Colleen, and she was happy. The first of the week, I was at the service station at 8:00 a.m. The station was already open, and they were pretty busy. The personnel manager came in and introduced himself. He asked me about thirty question and then told me I had the job and that I would start training at that same location. He asked if I had any questions, and I said. "Yes sir, just one. It has been a long time since I filled out the form. How come it tool so long for you to call me?"

"well," he said "there are quite a few reasons. We are in the process of changing our logo from American Oil to Amoco, and that involves a lot of traveling on our part-going from station to station and talking to dealers about changing their overhead sign and the names of out product. So we have been going from dealer to dealer. We went to one our operators up in Windsor Mill Road, and the owner talked so much about how good you are that I just wanted to talk to you and see for myself."

I said, "Well, I hope you won't be disappointed."

He said, "I'm not."

On my way home, I stopped at Phil's station and told him, "Thanks for the vote of confidence." I worked full-time at the Amoco Station for two years and was made manager, but I was still looking for something. I did not know what! Colleen's mother and father had decided to move back to the city. She was doing better physically, and Pop could find more work closer to the city. So they bought a house on Hemlock Avenue in Hamilton. Then Colleen decided that we should move, I told her, "We can't afford to move every time your mom and dad move."

She told me, "That's not the reason I want to move, but with them gone, who's going to help me with the baby?"

I said, "Stop calling him a baby. He's almost six years old."

She said, with a smile on her face, "Not him. The new one that's on the way."

My mouth fell open. I was speechless. Finally, I asked her, "When did you find out?"

She said, "The week before Mom and Dad moved." So, there we were that night, sitting in the living room on the couch. The TV was on, and I leaned over to her and said, "What do you want? A boy or a girl?"

She said, "We already have a boy. I think I would like to have a girl."

"OK," I said, "let's pick out girls names only, and then it will definitely be a girl."

She said, "We were just lucky the last time. God might have a different opinion."

I said, "No, it will work. We just pick out all-girls names."

"Now just name a few girls names, and we'll see," she said. "I already have a name picked out if it's a girl and if you if agree."

"What is it?" I asked.

She replied, "Jeaney Marie."

I said, "That sounds beautiful to me. One little girl coming up in nine months."

Now while we were waiting for blessed event number two, Colleen found a house down in the southern Baltimore called Harendale. There was a house for sale with three bedrooms, a living room, a dining room, a kitchen, and a carport with toolshed right outside the kitchen door. Just perfect. In the meantime, I had been working at a Gulf station on York Road and Woodborn Avenue right door to a Food Fair store in Govanstown. The station was owned by two partners, Don and Jimmy. While I was working there, a man I did not know and whose name I cannot remember at this time came up to me and said, "How much money do you make here in a week?"

I told him, "Not to be rude, but I don't think that's any of your business."

He said, "I wanted to know because I want to offer you a job where you can make double what you make in a week." He talked. I listened.

I gave Don and Jimmy a week's notice, and the next week I started at Butler Roofing Company. The man took me to an area where there were quite a few houses. He said. "All you have to do is rap on doors and tell people that you are selling aluminum siding and roofing. You would like to make an appointment to come back in the evening and talk to the husband and wife at the same time."

And then he said, "I'll be back here at five o'clock to pick you up." So off he went. That first day I don't know how many doors I knocked on, but at the end of the day, I had four appointments. When he came to pick me up at five o'clock and I told him I had four appointments, he said "That's great! You made forty dollars today. Could you make money like that in one day in a service station?"

I replied, "No, sir."

He said he would pick me up at the shop at 8:00 a.m. the next day. We drove to the same area that I worked the day before. So I started canvasing the houses. At lunchtime I only had three scheduled visits for him that night. By the time five o'clock rolled around, I had four more. I had a total of seven for the day. He said, "I don't know what you are doing, but keep on doing it."

Things were going good. I thought to myself, *If I can get these appointments, why can't I just make the sales?* I would have to ask. The next day on my way to work, my car broke down, and I had to call the office so my sales manager would not wait for me. The next day he called my house. "I'll pick you up and take you back home at the end of the day." We worked together that day, and he asked if I would like to go on a daytime sales call with him. Of course, I said yes. After all, he had the car. The husband and wife were both at home, and as we arrived, the man of the house opened the door and invited us in. we all sat down in their living room. The salesman asked what they were interested in. they replied aluminum siding. He said, "Let us go outside and get some measurements, and we will see what we can work out."

He and I went outside. It was not quite dark, so we could see the marks on the tape measure. First, the length; second, the width; third, the height. Count the number of windows, measure them to the inside frame, subtract the that amount from the total cost of the siding, and there you have your cost. "But," he said, "you don't tell the customer that price." He also told me, "When you have the length and the width of the house, you also have the footage for the roof. All you have to do is double it."

We went back inside, sat down, and he wrote all the figures for the aluminum siding. The people talked back and forth for about ten minutes and finally said they were happy with the price, and then he said, "OK, but for another five hundred dollars, I'll throw in an aluminum roofing!"

The couple were extremely happy and asked when we could start. He said, "There is some paperwork that you will have to sign. Wesley here will bring it to you the day after tomorrow, and we will probably start that following Monday with two crews-one on the siding and one on the roof. And if you get any referrals from any of your neighbors, Wesley will see you get a bonus check for fifty dollars." We left.

He said, "Well, what do you think?"

I said, "That's great, but where am I going to get this fifty-dollar referral fee from?"

He said, "Don't worry. It is in an account at the office as soon as the work is done and the bank pays off. And by the way, take tomorrow off but don't go out till after one o'clock."

So the next day, as I waited for one o'clock to come, a nice four door green-colored car parked in front of the house. I thought, *Boy, they have some nerve.* Then the doorbell rang, and there was my salesman standing there holding some car keys in his hand.

He said, "How do you like your new car?"

I could not believe it. I said, "I can't afford to buy a car like that!"

"Relax," he said. "The money to make the car payments will come out of your account that the company holds for you after each sale you make." So things were really going great. Things went well.

For the next three months, I was working almost every night making two to three sales per night. Colleen was getting upset because I working so much at night. Sometimes I would not get home till eleven or after midnight. She thought I had found a girlfriend or was just having a fling with another woman. Well, she delivered the baby, and again, I was not there at her bedside when she delivered a beautiful healthy baby girl. We already picked out her name-Tammy Jean.

So time went by, and I was still working a lot of nights, coming home late and listening to Colleen yell and complain. So finally, I had enough.

I quit my job and started looking in the paper again. Sure enough, God did supply my need. In the paper was an ad for a service station attendant. I applied, got the job, and started the next day. The Exxon station was next door to a small store that sold hotdogs and ice cream. The name of the shop was the Dog House. Colleen said to me, "You get to go out and work all day and get to talk to other people. All I do is stay home and do the housework and take care of the kids. I want to get a job where I get a paycheck each week." So one day she picked up the kids, walk from where we lived, and got a job-where else but at the Dog House. I would go to work in the morning and work from 7:00 a.m. to 5:00 p.m., then come home, and the she would go to work at 6:00 p.m. and work till twelve midnight, then come home.

I don't know if it helped or not, but in a few weeks, she said to me, "Honey, guess what?"

I said, "What?"

She said, "I'm pregnant."

I said, "Great! What do we want this time?"

She said, "Well we have one boy and one girl, and as far as I know there is no other choice. But it would be nice if we had another girl so they could grow up together."

So went down and picked out all-girl names. She said, "We were lucky last time. God heard our prayer and gave us one boy and one girl. Do you think it will work again?"

I said, "I'm not very religious, but when you got a good thing going, don't mess with it."

So we picked out all-girls names, and on February 20, 1958, Cindy Lou appeared.

Things went along pretty good. But I was not making enough money where I was, so I went back to the Gulf station. When I got there, Don told me that he and Jimmy had had a disagreement and that Jimmy had sold his interest to Don. I jumped for joy, asked, and got a job making two dollars more than I currently was. I worked there for two months, and then one of the executive from Food Fair came over and asked me if I would like to work at Food Fair. I said yes. He didn't tell me anything about the job I was being offered, and I didn't ask.

Two weeks after that I walked into the store next to the gas station

I had worked at. The first day I filled out an employment application-an application to join the meat cutters union and an application for health insurance. I was all set. The store manager came to me and asked me a question that never expected. "What do you know about fish?"

I thought for a minute and said, "I know that they swim in water and some people catch them with a hook." Now I know that Jesus told his apostles, "Follow me, and I will make you a man of fishes." So I started working behind the seafood counter waiting on customers. I had a three-month training course (that's how long it took to get the money to join the union out of my paycheck). I learned how to weigh fish and clean them, how to tell the difference in shrimp, how to fillet a flounder, how to tell the difference between clams and oysters, how to cook chickens on the rotisseries, and how to order and make gefilte fish. The headman for Food Fair stores in the Baltimore/Washington area was Mr. Wolf. While I was training and even after, he used to come around and inspect all the departments. One day he walked by the counter and looked at the display in the seafood case and asked me, "Who set up the display?"

I replied, "I did."

He said, "You must be a real epholigest!"

I said, "what's that?"

He said, "When you learn that, then you are one." Then he left the store.

CHAPTER 9

(The New Beginning)???

Thirty days after my union dues were paid, it was official, and I was a seafood clerk. At the end of my time, I was working on the inventory in the fish cooler when the seafood merchandiser came in and said, "Wesley, we are going to move you." I thought to myself, *Good, I can get out of this stinking fish department.*

He said, "Effective Monday morning, you report to the Food Fair store on Ritchie Highway."

I was a little disappointed, but God works in mysterious ways. His wisdom to behold! I said, "OK, but who do I report to?"

He said, "Harvy York. He's the store manager. You are his new seafood manager."

Well, I was shocked! Me? Why me? How can I be promoted so quick? It must be a mistake. Monday morning came, and I drove down Ritchie Highway till I saw a sign that read Harundale Mall, and right under that sign was the entrance to the Food Fair store. It was the only mall that I had ever seen with a food market for an anchor store.

I went in and went up to the office and told the lady in charge who I was and that I was there to see Mr. York. She picked up the loudspeaker and paged Mr. York to the office. Now over the three months I had been with Food Fair, I heard from different meat managers and others about how tough of the store managers were. Mr. York's name was at the top. He came to the office, looked at me, and said, "You must be my seafood manager. What's your name?"

"Wesley," I said.

"Do you have a last name?" he asked.

I thought, *Oh boy, I'm off to a good start.*

"How long have you been a seafood manager?" he asked. When I said that this was my first store, I could read the disappointment in his face. I went to work setting up the seafood counter and putting ice in the roll-way ice table that went in front of the seafood counter for crabmeat. I also put chickens on the rotisserie to start them cooking.

One day we got a notice that a special price and sale for rockfish was going to be held and that company officials would be touring the stores and judging the displays, I had a brainstorm. I talked to one of the cashiers who I knew and asked her to knit me a small dress and a shirt and a pair of pants. She did. I went to the five-and-ten cents store in the mall and bought the two little hats. When the promotion came out in newspaper it was for "dressed rockfish = twenty-nine cents a pound." I put the shirt and pants on one fish and the dress on another and sat them up in the seafood case. The company representatives came in and looked at the display, and the next week I was awarded my first E for Excellence award along with a check for twenty-five dollars. Colleen, in the meantime, was busy taking care of the kids. One evening when I came home from work and went into the basement to change my clothes and rinse off the fish smell, she met me at the top of the stairs and said, "Guess what?"

I said, "What?"

She said, I'm pregnant."

I looked at her and said, "How do you know?"

She said, "I went to the doctor today because I thought I might be. He did some tests, and I was right. We are going to have another baby!"

I did not believe her and sent her to see another doctor, and he confirmed the first doctor's diagnosis. When she told me, I found another doctor and sent her to him. It was the same result. We were going to have another child. Once again, we started to talk about what we wanted. Again, we turned to the formula we had used in the past. We picked out all-boys names. And once again, God was working in our lives. On November 1, 1960, Timothy Michael came into our lives.

Everything seemed to be going well for us, but then something happened that really tested our faith. Cindy, our youngest daughter, was playing outside with another little girl. They had found a couple of broken-off sticker bush limbs and were running and waving them around when one of the bushes hit Cindy in the eye. She went into the house crying and holding her hand over her eye. Colleen looked at it and used some hot towels on the eye to help stop hurting. It did not work. She took Cindy in the car to an eye specialist who was close by. He examined her eye and said, "The thorn is still in her eye. I'll try to remove it." He worked on the eye for what Colleen said "seemed like hours." And finally, he got the thorn out. He prescribed some eye drops and put a patch over Cindy's damaged eye. Later on that evening, Cindy started crying. We asked her what was wrong. She replied, "My eye hurts really, really bad." It was late. The doctor was closed. There was nothing else to do but go to the hospital. We put her in the car. The other kids were asleep. So Colleen said, "I will take her to the hospital. You stay with the other children because I know what the doctor did and you don't." So into the car they went, and off they drove.

Time passed by very slowly. I kept thinking, *Why is she taking so long? Why doesn't call?* Hours went by. The whole time I was sitting in the chair, worrying. I did not give a thought to prayer. Finally, I heard the car pull up in the driveway, and Colleen got out, went around to the passenger side, and brought Cindy out and into the house. Colleen put her to bed, then came out to the living room with me.

She said, "The hospital called in an eye specialist. He worked on the eye for about half an hour and then told me she was going to need an operation. He said that the bad eye was infected and because of the way the eyes work, if he did not operate, she could lose the sight in her good eye. Then the doctor said she is already blind in the damaged eye."

Colleen said, "What could I do? I told the doctor to operate." With that statement, she fell into my arms, crying. I tried to calm her down, holding back my tears at the same time and thinking, *Why, Lord? Why did you let this happen?* I never did get an answer.

Time went on. Cindy had lost the sight in her one eye, and when school started up, a lot of the kids asked why she had two different-colored eyes. Cindy came home from school crying because of what they said. Colleen would take her in her arms, hug her, and hold Cindy's head close to her own heart. Finally, one day when Cindy came home again crying, Colleen told Cindy, "The next time at school or any place else when somebody asks you why you have different colored eyes, just say 'I was kissed by and angel!'" Cindy liked that idea, and when she told people that, she was happy and smiled.

Things moved along. We had a bad season for fish one year, and fresh fish was in short supply. The advertising department went to promoting frozen fish products. Now Mr. York, the store manager that everyone said was hard to get along with and also hard to work for, came to me and asked if I had any ideas on how to promote frozen seafood products. I said, "Let me work on it." The next day I went into the mall and talked to the manager of a children's clothing store. I asked if he had a manikin of a boy that he could lend to me for a month. He looked at me like I had lost my mind. He had one that he had not planned to use for a while and said I would be welcome to use it. I also bought a white pullover shirt, a pair of blue shorts, a pair of white socks, and a pair of tennis shoes. I also bought a white sailor's cap. I put on them on the boy, stood him in the frozen food freezer case, borrowed a fishing rod from the meat manager, and made up a sign to hang over the manikin's head that read "Captain York's Delight is right when the fish won't bite." It won me another E award and a nice cash prize. It also got a promotion for Mr. York to a new store in a larger section of Anne Arundel County. A few weeks later, I was transferred to that store. Things were going along fine, and summer was coming on.

It was time for Colleen to start her southern migration. Every year as soon as school was over, she would pack up our pop-up camper and take them to Assateague Park that is located near Ocean City, Maryland. The reason she did this was because June 23 was her birthday. She always said that she did not like birthdays and that if she took the kids camping during that week, they would not remember her birthday, and therefore, she did not have a birthday and did not get older. Now for some reason I do not know and cannot explain, Colleen was very jealous of me around other women. When I had jobs where I was out working at night, she would think I was with another woman. She would say something, and we would have a disagreement. This went on for years and years. One time she asked me how I wanted to be buried when I died. I told her I wanted to be cremated. She said, "That's good, but if I die before you do, I want to be cremated too."   I said to her, "I'm glad to hear that."

She said, "Why?"

I told her, "Because you have been burning me up for years, and this is my chance to get even.

One day while I was working behind the seafood counter, two men approached and asked if I was Wes Watts. I said "I am. How can I help you?"

One of the men said, "We represent Amoco Oil Company, and we have heard that you would to operate your own service station. Is that true?"

I said, "Yes, sir."

He said, "When can we get together and talk?"

I said, "Any night after work, If you would like to come to the house, we could talk after dinner."

They asked, "Would tonight be too soon?"

I replied, "No, sir, tonight would be fine. Say between six thirty and seven?"

They said, "Fine, see you then," and left.

I had told Colleen that two men were coming to talk to us about opening our own service station. She said, "How much is it going to cost?"

I said "I don't know. That's what they are coming here for."

Six thirty came, and the doorbell rang. Colleen took the children upstairs and them to play up there till she came up to get them. Meanwhile, I answered the door and invited them in. I said we could go into the kitchen to talk because the light was better and we could all sit around the table. Colleen came in, and we all sat around the table. We talked about what I knew about service station work, how I first got started, and finally, the big question.

"How much money do you have in the bank?" they asked.

I told them, "About six hundred dollars."

They said, "Well, that isn't very much to start with, but I think we can help. If you will give us a commitment tonight that you are willing to go to school for two weeks to learn the bookkeeping part of the business, we would be willing to help you get started."

I asked Colleen, "What do you think?"

She said, "You have to make this decision yourself. You're the one who is going to have to put in the long hours." I turned to the two men and said, "If I can have two weeks to give notice to Food Fair, you've got a deal."

They said, "OK, in two weeks you report to our training class. It is located on Harford Road, and they will teach you the paperwork and how to the bookwork. You will have to hire a bookkeeper so you can keep track for tax purposes."

Now do you remember from the beginning of this book the one word when I was in the gas station pretending to put gas in my tricycle? The word *wait*. Was this what God wanted me to wait for?

God works in mysterious ways, his miracles to behold.

CHAPTER 10

A New Way of Life!

Well, the two weeks went by. I left the seafood counter behind and opened a new chapter in life. The following Monday, I reported to the Amoco training school on Harford Road. In two weeks, I knew the bookmark and how to keep track of inventory. On the last day of school, the same two men who had talked to me at the Foodd Fair came in and took me to lunch. They told me they had two stations that they needed to have dealers for. The first one was on Greenmount Avenue side and one on the Twenty-Fifth Street side. Both islands had one regular and one premium gas pump. The station office was back away from the pumps, and alongside the office were four service bays. Now this station I knew pretty well because it was an area I traveled past while I was growing up. The other station was over on the opposite side of town located at Cold Spring Lane. This was very small station, and it just had one gas island and, next to the office, two service bays. One bay had a lift to raise a car up, and the other bay was used to wash cars. They said this station had been operated by one person from Amoco Oil Co. who only opened the station from 9:00 a.m. to 5:00 p.m. I think it surprised them when I said, "I'll take the small station."

So on June 6, 1966, I put the key in the door and opened Wes's Amoco. The price sign had the prices that read "Regular at 18.9 cents per gallon" and "Premium at 28.9 cents per gallon." I figured I would start small, grow big. I opened the station at 7:00 a.m. and closed at 10:00 p.m. Meanwhile, Colleen went to work for Food Fair. She started out as a cashier; met her best friend, Carol; and was promoted to office help.

Things were slow for the first two weeks. My sales representative came in one day and said, "You're going to need oil, tires, batteries, grease, some accessories, and some tire patches and repairs." I told him I could not afford any of that.

He said, "Don't worry, we'll put you in a small amount, and after you are opened three months, we'll give you sixty days pay off the bill. Plus we will give you your first load of gas free. You don't have to pay for the first load of gas till you get the second load."

I thought to myself, *What have I gotten into?*

One day a lady drove her car in to get gas. When t greeted her, I said, "good morning, ma'am, would you like to fill your tank today?"

She said, "Yes, fill it up please."

While the gas was being pumped into the tank through the automatic nozzle, I asked if I could check under the hood. She said yes, and I raised the hood pulled out the oil dipstick, and saw that the oil was clean. I checked the power steering fluid and the battery and coolant level. I closed the hood, went to the driver's side window, and said, "Your oil and all your Fluids look OK at this time." She thanked me. I topped off the fuel tank. I then got some paper towels and spray bottle and washed her front and back window and told her how much her gas cost.

She paid and asked, "How long have you worked here?"

I replied, "I just started today."

She said, "I thought you must be new. The other fellow acts like it's too much trouble to even put gas in, I certainly hope you stay around for a while."

I assured her I would be. The next day I was unlocking the gas pumps, a customer pulled in, and before I could say anything, he got out of the car and asked, "Are you the person who waited on my wife yesterday?"

So replied, "I'm the only one here, sir, so I guess I was."

He said, "she told me how helpful you were, and I just wanted to thank you."

I said, "Well, thank you, sir. And thank you for coming by to tell me."

He said, "Do you have radio to listen to inside?"

I said, "Sometimes." He was getting back into his car when he said, "Listen at ten o'clock a voice came over the radio and said, "Good morning, listeners, I want to tell you an experience that my wife had at a gas station yesterday." And he went on to tell his listeners all about his wife's experience and about our little talk that morning. He also said that he would be going to that station when his car needed gas or service. Then he said, "This station 1300, and this is your host on the morning show, Bailiey Goss." I was totally blown away. He and his wife started coming in on a regular basis, and the new business took off.

The station had been pumping about six to eight hundred gallons of gas a day. At the end of the first week, our daily gallon use was 1,200 too 1,300 a day. Service work was starting to come in, and I needed some help. School was out, so our son came over to help out. He worked every day with me. The hours were getting too long, so I hired another person that I knew from another station. His name was Vince. One day while I was alone at the station, a man that I knew from another station that I had worked at came walking through the front door and said, "Wes! Do you need a good mechanic?"

I thought he was kidding and said, "Yes, do you know where I can get one?"

He replied, "Yes, me."

I said, "Rudy, I would love to have you working here, but there is no way I can afford to pay you what you want to make."

Rudy said, "I'll make you a good deal. I'll come in Monday through Friday at eight in the morning until five at night. I'll sit right here on this deacon's bench, and when a car pulls in. I'll tell you what it needs in the way of motor repair. If you sell the work, I'll do it, and the only thing you pay me is one half of the labor and five percent of the parts."

I could not believe it. Had no reason to take advantage of Rudy's offer. The very next day a car pulled in, and the driver said, "Fill it up with regular."

"Yes, sir," I said and started to check under the hood. I went to the gas pump, shut it off, closed the gas tank, and told the driver, "If you start the engine, I'll check your transmission. He did, and I checked. it was full. I closed the hood, went to the driver's window, and told him the cost of his gas. He handed me a credit card. I went inside to put the card through the machine, and Rudy, who was sitting on the deacon's bench, said, "That car needs a tune-up."

I said, "How do you know that?"

He said, "I'm the mechanic. When you go back to the car, ask him if he has a problem starting his car on damp or cold mornings."

I took the credit card back to the customer. While he was signing for the credit card, I asked the customer the question Rudy had told me to ask. I came back in to Rudy and said, "I did just like you told me, and he asked what a tune-up would cost."

Rudy said, "Tell him between fifty to seventy-five dollars, depending on what parts he needs when we look at them."

I told the driver, and he drove away. I came back into the office.

Rudy said, "When is he bringing the car in?"

I said, "Day after tomorrow, but how did you know he said yes?"

Rudy said, "The look on your face gave you away."

I said, "OK, smarty, but what you don't know is that he wants a lube, oil, and oil filter change too."

Well, things were going pretty good. Then the gas shortage of 1972 came about. The Middle East was holding back on oil production, so gasoline became scarce. The company said we were only allowed to sell a certain amount of gallons each day. They gave us notice of how each month. It was up to us to determine how much gas we wanted to pump each day. But they warned us that when the allotment was gone there would be no more delivered till the following month. I stuck the tanks in the ground every day and divided that by the number of days we would be open that month, figuring on closing on all holidays. Then every hour I would stick the tanks, and if it was getting to close to the limit, I started to only sell ten gallons per car. Thank God that shortage did last too long. We had lines lined up on both sides of the pumps coming in and lining up on the curb side of Cold Spring Lane. From the other direction, cars would line up over the hill. So about three hours before it was close to our limit, I would send Cindy one way with a sign that read "Last car in line. No more gas for sale today." I told her to hold her sign up so no cars would be getting in line behind her. I also had Tim hold up the same sign for the people coming from over the hill. While I was sticking the tanks every hour, I could estimate just how long cars should be at the pumps.

One day I realized that I should be able to see the last car, and it was not in sight. Tammy and Ken were pumping gas; Buddy and I were checking under the hoods. I asked Rudy to take my place and see the nobody tried to jump in line, and then I walked down the street just in time to see Cindy take something from a driver and move the sign back behind that car. I asked her what she was doing. She answered, "Tim said we could each make some extra money if we would just let one or two cars a day in line after you said last car." I could not say too much with the customer there. But that evening when we closed the station and got home, neither one liked it when I took away all the extra money that day. After that they still went to the end of the lines with their signs, but I went along too and wrote down the license plate number and the type and color of the car.

One morning I went in a little earlier to catch up on some paperwork. I was shocked to see a Volkswagen locked up and sitting in front of the gas pump on the inside pump. I went into the office thinking the person might slipped a note and the car key the door. No such luck. There was no key. Six o'clock came and went. Cars were lining up behind the Volkswagen and on the outside of the pumps, waiting for me to turn the lights on and start pumping gas. I thought the only right thing I could do was start the car on the outside pumping, hold the second car back, take the front car on the inside lane, and just keep that going until the owner of the Volkswagen came back.

Buddy came in to work, I explained what was going on and told him to do it that way till I got back. He took over, and I walked up the hill and found four big strong-looking men and offered them a deal. "If you four men will come down to the station and help Buddy and me move a Volkswagen away from the inside pumps, when you come down with your cars, I will give you fifteen gallons instead of ten gallons." They agreed, and the six of us picked up the Volkswagen and moved it over to where there was a small wall at the property line. We sat the on that wall. We finally got the cars moving again.

At about seven thirty, the owner of the Volkswagen came walking into the station. "What did you do to my car?" he screamed.

I said, "Is that it over there?"

He said, "How did you move it? I did not leave the key."

I said, "When I opened up this morning, I told the people in that line they would have to wait till I got all the cars in the outside out before I could take them because your car had the pumps block. A few minutes later four big men came down and picked your car up and moved it over there."

He said, "You are going to have to get it down for me!"

"I've got customers to serve, I don't have time to fool with you now," I said. He left, and about a half hour later, he came back in a police car with a policeman. The policeman came over to me and tasked me what happened. After I explained, the man with the Volkswagen said, "The station was closed, and I did not see why I could not park where I wanted to."

The policeman looked at him and said, "When this station is open, it is open to the public. But when it is closed, it is private property, and you can't park on someone else's property. if Mr. Watts wants me to, I will be forced to give a parking ticket."

I said, "Thanks anyway, but let's just let it go."

The man said, "But what about my car? How am I going to get it down?"

I said, "Call a tow truck. There's a phone inside the office if you want to use it." He did. The tow truck came, and in a half hour, the Volkswagen and its driver were history.

Meanwhile, time was passing by. Our son Ken had had started a band, and the band had a girl named Pat. Ken and Pat started dating when there was no band gigs. And before we knew it, Pat and Ken got married. They were married on January 1971. They have two boys named Richard (born December 5, 1972) and Shawn (born November 1973). Richard has two children-a boy named Austin and a girl named Haley. Shawn has four boys. Our eldest daughter, Tammy Jean, is married to her husband, Dan, and they were married on February 14, 1978. I have one granddaughter named Jenny who was born on August 23, 1979, and one grandson named Clay born on January 21, 2001. Our youngest daughter, Cindy, married to Doug. They have no children yet. Our youngest son, Tim, is married.

Colleen loved to travel. On our fifth wedding anniversary, she said, "I don't expect to live till our twenty-fifth wedding anniversary, and I would like to go to Hawaii." So we went. She also said, "I don't think I'll live to celebrate our fiftieth wedding anniversary." So on our tenth anniversary, we went to the Holy Land.

The Holy Land Trip

We flew from Baltimore to Chicago and from Chicago to San Francisco. When we arrived in San Francisco, we had to wait until evening before our plane was to leave. We had heard of the cab rides up and down the streets on San Francisco, so we decided to try one. It was quite an experience, and everything we had heard about it was true. It was getting to be evening, and we decided to tour Fisherman's Wharf. Everything we had heard about that place was also true. We found a restaurant that had a revolving restaurant on top of it, and we decided to try it. We were surprised while we were eating dinner because on stage was a singer named Rudy Valley. He sang, we ate, and the singing actually helped make the taste better. By the time we finished eating, it was time to get back to the airport. The cab ride back to the airport didn't to much to hold the good dinner down. Thank God it wasn't any longer.

When we got to the airport it was just about boarding time. We got in line, and I don't know how or why Colleen and I were picked to sit in the front section of the airplane. The plane took off just about twilight. We were on our way to Israel, the home where Jesus actually walked and worked and lived and died. So we all would be able to see the place where Jesus lived. When we reached our cruising altitude, we could look out the window and see the lights of the city just coming on. And if we looked up, above the airplane, it was still light. It was a beautiful sight of God's handiwork to behold. We cruised through the night, dosing off to sleep for a few minutes, then waking up to look out the window and see the lights on the wings. And then we would fall back to sleep. Just before dawn, the flight attendant came around with coffee and doughnuts. They also did not want us to miss it when the sun came through the darkness. What a sight! Beautiful!

We landed at the airport and we were taken into two different buildings by armed military. This brought us all back to reality. The military people took us into small rooms, and there we were told to remove all clothing. Then our clothing was searched, and we were checked thoroughly! After we were allowed to dress, we were taken to another building where our ID from the airport was checked with our luggage tags. Colleen had her hand camera with her, and she said that to make sure it was really a camera, the two men took pictures of each other. Meanwhile, two men were checking my suitcase. Inside was an eight-millimeter movie camera. They saw it and thought it was a gun because it had a trigger. It took twenty minutes to find an Israeli who could understand English and explain to the two Israelis that it took moving pictures.

Well, we finally got through security and were taken by bus to the hotel we would be staying at for the next three days. We were taken into a reception room at the hotel, and an Arab who could speak our language spoke to us about security. He said that for security purposes, we should not leave the hotel after dark. When we met with the leader of the group, who just happened to be our preacher, we were to give him our passports. He would be responsible for our passports. Whenever we were stopped by security, he would have to show your passport so they could verify that you were with the group. By this time, it was late, and we just decided to go to bed.

The next day we were taken by bus to the place where the Dead Sea scrolls were found. From there we went to the Dead Sea. We got off the bus and were given half an hour to explore and cast stones into the Dead Sea. Some people threw a shoe into the sea to see if that would really float. It did and went farther and farther out to sea. The person in charge of our group said, "You may as well through the other shoe in too because the other will probably never come back." We also went to the Garden of Gethsemane where Jesus prayed, "Father, if it is possible let this task pass from me. Nevertheless, Father, no my will be done, but thine," and blood fell on the ground.

Now it was late, so on the way back to the hotel, the preacher announced that that evening after dinner, anyone who would like to come into the meeting room after we ate could discuss the events of the day and have a prayer service after. The pastor never came to that meeting. The next day was the day everyone was looking forward to! We were going into the walled city of Jerusalem. We would walk the path Jesus walked when he carried the cross to Calvary. The street was called Straight. We walked that street, and the shops and stores on both sides had lamb and oxen other supplies hanging outside on hooks, just like Jesus's day. We could look ahead and see the hill called Calvary straight ahead. Some already had tears in their eyes. Some were already crying. Some were still holding back all emotions. We walked up to a viewing stand that had been built because the government would not let people climb Mount Calvary. They were afraid visitors might destroy the hill by digging for souvenirs or hoping to find a buried cross or something else. You can stand on the viewing platform and see the spot where the three crosses stood or walk around the other side of the platform and see the skull that is mentioned in the Garden. Then after we left there, we went through what looked like a small garden and came to a tomb that was dug into the side of the mountain.

And there on the right-hand side of the path was the opening. The entrance to the tomb where the body of Jesus, the Lord and the Christ, was laid for three days! It was where the three women spoke with the angel, where Peter and John ran to but still did not understand. Now there were people going in and coming out. Colleen went in before me. I waited until almost everyone else had gone in and had come out. I stopped, bowed my head, and there on the inside of the cave was a long flat ledge. It looked like marble to me. I looked and I looked. I turned to leave, and as I exited through the door, I felt water running down my face! Was I crying? I should be happy, not sad! The tomb is still empty! How can I be crying? Then I realized that because the tomb is empty, you know your savior lives! Then outside the empty tomb, the pastor, gave everyone Holy Communion. What a beautiful way to end the day.

The next day we got on a boat and sailed on the Sea of Galilee. The driver of the boat stopped about halfway, and we just sat there for at least half an hour. We started up again and landed on the opposite side. We visited the dome where the rock that Jesus prayed on was supposed to be. We visited the garden where Jesus prayed to the Father "Father, if It be possible, let this thing pass from me. Nevertheless not my will but thine be done." We walk back to the boat and went back across. We went to our hotel and started to pack because we were heading for Rome, Italy, next.

The next day at Rome the whole bunch wanted to visit the Vatican. We were a lot of first timers to visit Rome, including Colleen and me. We entered St. Peter's Cathedral. There was a very large statue of St. Peter on the right side of the entrance. A lot of people stopped long enough to kiss the feet of the statue. We saw the original painting on the ceiling of the last supper. We went by the pope's living quarters. It was guarded by two guards dressed in clothing of that era and armed with swords and spears.

After that we all went to eat lunch for an hour. After lunch we got on a bus, and the driver took us to the remains of the Coliseum and other places.

The next day we got on the airplane and were given back our passports. And then we flew to a part of Germany called the Rhineland. We spent about four hours there, then got on another airplane and headed for home, the good old USA; and where did we land? Las Vegas. That seemed kind of odd to me, from paradise to Sin City. But maybe that was just my thinking. We spent the rest of that day seeing how much money we could leave there. (Colleen won five hundred dollars.) we boarded the plane and took off at just about six thirty. As we were flying, we could see the lights of Las Vegas flashing on and off, and as we flew higher, we could see complete darkness above and still light below. We landed in Chicago only to find out that the flight we were supposed to be on was overbooked. The announcer for the airlines said anyone willing to give up their seats could be scheduled on the next-day flight, and because of the inconvenience, the airlines would pay for a hotel room that night and give two free tickets to fly to any other state and also provide free dinner and breakfast at the café. We were not in any particular hurry to get home, so we took the offer.

The next day we returned to work. Ken (our son) said everything went OK while we were gone. No problems. *Great,* I thought. When a few days went by, Rudy, the mechanic, came to work and said he wanted to talk to me. He had met a lady he really liked. She worked as a cab driver, and they had fallen in love with each other. They were going to get married. But she had family that lived in Costa Mesa, California; and they would be moving to California. What could I say? I told Rudy we all wished him and Hilda all the best and that we would miss him. Then to quote the Bible, I said, "The Lord giveth, and the Lord taketh away. Blessed be the name of the Lord."

My supervisor from Amoco came and said, "Wes, the company would like to know if you would be interested in taking over a larger station to operate?"

I said, "Probably, yes, I would. Where is this other station located?"

"It's over on East Cold Spring Lane," he said.

"You mean that location that has three gas islands and five bays?"

"That's the one," he said.

"How soon would I have to let you know?" I asked.

He said, "By tomorrow."

"OK," I said. that night Colleen, Ken, and I all sat down to talk about it. Later I prayed.

"The decision is yours," Colleen said.

The next day when Len (the Amoco man) came in, I said, "I am thinking I would like to take over that location, but what will you do with this station?"

"Well," Len said "probably after you move out, we will close it down."

I said, "I don't think that's very fair to all the customers here. Why can't I keep it open and operate both?"

He said, "It's against company policy for one operator to operate two locations, and besides that we only lease this property. And the lease is up in December, and we are not going to renew it.

I thought for a few minutes. (I knew already that I was going to take the larger location, but I didn't want to look to anxious.) I said, "What kind of a deal is the company willing to offer me?"

Len said, "They will give you three months rent-free, twenty tires of various sizes, ten batteries, and fifty dollars' worth of accessories and tire patches."

I thought that was a pretty good deal, I said, "Len, that's a pretty good deal, but it's not good enough. Let's try this-everything the company has offered plus I get to deep this location until the thirty-first of December. That will give me time to get customers used to coming over to East Cold Spring Lane, and I can get Colleen, who has already been certified as a manager/operator, to run this location."

He said, "Let me run it by the company." Len came back the next day and said the company would take the deal I proposed except for one thing-the service bays would have to be closed and locked. I did not like that idea because that is where all my profit came from, but I agreed.

The next Sunday at church, the pastor came to me and said, "I would like to nominate you to be anointed as a deacon in the church. If you are elected, would you accept?" I said I would be honored but only if the vote was unanimous. The following Sunday the vote was taken. And the following Sunday at the evening service, I was sworn in as a church deacon. Now a church deacon was to be a leader in prayer, to visit with the congregation, to help the sick, and any other things that they were asked to do. Now as I took over the new station, I thought about how we could keep the customers from the old station and bring them to the new station. So I prayed and asked God for guidance. You know the verse in the Bible that says "ask and you shall receive. Seek and you shall find. Knock and it will be opened. For nothing is impossible with God."? Well, I prayed and I knocked and what do you know! The answer and God's Word came true!

I took Colleen and out her at the little station as manager. I put two full-time workers on day service and two part-time workers on night duty. I told them, "If any customers come in, let them leave their car and get the information of what they done to their vehicle and a phone number where they can be reached. Give them the keys to your car. After they leave, you call me and let me know the name, phone number, and what service they wanted. then have one of your workers drive the customer's car over here, leave it, and take my car back over to you incase you get another service job to done." This plan worked out very good until December.

Now Colleen and I had and I joined a Moose Lodge, and after about three months, the lodge voted for members to take positions on both male and female officers. Colleen was elected and rose up in positions over the years to senior regent, which she held for two years. I was elected to the men's committee and was elected to serve as chaplain. My duties were to say the opening and closing prayers. A question-could this have been what God meant when I was five years old and pretending to put gas into my tricycle and he said "wait"? Now things were coming into shape at the big station. People asked me, "What are you going to call the new location?" we decided to call it Cold Spring Amoco.

One day our church pastor came over just to see what sort of a service station we had. He stayed a while, and before he left, he asked me what I would like him to pray for. I said, "For happiness and goodwill among us all."

He prayed and then said, "I might as well fill up here before I leave."

He pulled up to the pump, and I went out to fill his tank and check under the hood. He reached for his wallet, and I told him, "Don't bother. That full tank is on us."

He said, "You don't get your gas for free. I don't expect to get my gas for free."

I told him about what had happened to me when I was five years old and when I heard the word *wait*. Now the new station had five service bays. The three bays all had lifts in them. The two bays on the side of the station had one that was just a flat floor, and the other was a pit that had five steps leading down into it. At the back of the three front bays was a fence that ran from the ceiling to the floor with one door on the front. It was a good area for storing tires as the three walls had the racks hanging on them all ready and plenty of room for storing batteries.

Along came 1974, another so-called gas shortage. This time the government made it easy for the station operators. They made a rule that on even-numbered days on the calendar, only vehicles with the last number on their license plates were to get gas, and on odd-numbered days, cars with odd numbers on their license plates were to get gas. But any doctor, firefighter, of police officer could get gas any day at any time-even if you had pumped your quota. Because we were a new station the company said they had nothing to go by, so our limit was unlimited. I asked the state representative when he came by to check as they did to see if we were following the limits. The pastor of our church came in to get gas. Now we had two driveways leading up to our gas pumps and three gas islands. So we put signs at the beginning of each driveway: "East entrance use gas island two. West entrance use gas island number one only." Now on the day the pastor came and the state inspector was there, I told the pastor to drive up to the first island as there was no waiting line there. When I had filled the pastor's vehicle and sent him on his way, the inspector asked me why I didn't ask for proof that that was an emergency vehicle. I said, "he is a church pastor. The law says I have to give prioritize doctors who don't even make house calls anymore. Now if you were home lying on your bed waiting to die, who would you want praying for you-the priest or clergyman or the doctor who cannot help you?"

Things were coming along very well at the new location. An older man came in one day and asked if I needed any help. I said, "What can you do?"

He said, "I am a mechanic."

I said, "What's your name, and when can you start?"

He said, "My name is Bill, and I start right now." I gave him an application and put him to work. It turned out he loved to do tune-ups and front-end alignments. Now there is a saying that says "G od works in mysterious ways, his miracles to behold." Guess what happened next?

Amoco sent around a notice that they were holding an equipment sale. Any dealer who attended would be eligible to win a trip-all-expenses paid-whether or not they bought equipment. I went to the show. They showed and demonstrated a new type of tire changer. I bought one on credit. They also said they would hook it up and demonstrate it to the other employees. They also demonstrated a new kind of scope machine that when hooked to a car engine, showed just what was needed on a tune-up. It came with the showing and showed how it operated to two employees at different times. I bought one. Now it came time to draw the ticket for the free trip to Santa Domenica.

"Where is that?" I asked the dealer sitting next to me.

"I never heard of it" he said.

I asked, "Who in their right mind would want to win a trip to a place that they don't even know where it is?" I got my answer sooner than I expected. They picked my name. I must have had at least fifteen people ask me to sell them the tickets. They went as high as five hundred dollars each. I was tempted, but I held off. Later Colleen and I took that trip. Santa Domenica is an island. The grave of Christopher Columbus is there also. We had a great time.

When we got back the equipment was being installed. First the front-end machine was installed. Bill was as happy as he could be. He did anywhere between three and five alignments in a day. He liked Chrysler cars best because almost everyone need an idler arm and he was being paid a commission on every he sold. The tire machine was next. That was pretty easy to work. We had it bolted down inside the cage where the tires were being kept. When it came to the tune-up machine that took a little longer to install because when they asked what bay I wanted it in, I said, "All three." The installer said he had never installed one that moved. I said, "There 's a first time for everything." It took the company about three weeks to figure out how to hook a rail so that the machine could move back and forth across the three bays. They did it.

Things were going great. Business was growing, and everything was falling in place. One day a customer asked if we did transmission work. Now one of my son -in-law had taken auto transmission service at Mervo Tech School. I told the customer yes but that we would have take the pan off the transmission and drain the oil before we could check to see what had to be replaced, so there would be a charge of thirty-five dollars to check and service it. He agreed to the price. The next day he brought the car in. I drove him to work, got his name and phone number, and told him I would call him when we found out what was wrong. Now on my way back, I stopped at a regular transmission shop and asked the person there if he could check the transmission for me. He said he could but that it would take him an hour before he could get to it. I told him who I was and where I was from and asked if he had any way to get me back to the station. He gave me the keys to his car and said, "You will need a way back when you come pick up the car." He called about an hour and a half after I left with some bad news. Yes, he could repair the transmission, but the whole transmission should be replaced. He told me it would cost seventy-five dollars for transmission fluid, caskets, and filters. I asked him what it would cost to rebuild the old transmission. He said he had one in stock to rebuild the old transmission. He said he had one in stock that would fit that car, and seeing as I was a service station operator, he would give me a discount and the transmission would cost me two hundred and twelve dollars. It would be guaranteed parts and labor for one year. I said, "How long to replace it?"

He said, "I can have it ready in two days."

I said, "I'll call you back." I called the customer and told him what the transmission man told me. He asked what the cost was. I told him seventy-five dollars to check it or three hundred and twelve dollars to replace it with a one-year guarantee. To my surprise, he said, "Go ahead and fix it. How long before I can pick it up?"

I said, "It will take two days, and then it will be ready."

He said, "OK. I'll get my brother to pick up me up and drop me off. See you in two days. Thank you! Goodbye."

I told one of the men to follow me over to the transmission shop so I could return the transmission man's car. I told him to go ahead and replace the transmission and that I would pick up the car up in two days. And then I asked how should I make out the check. He told me, and he said, "Any other transmission work you get in if you bring it to me, I'll give you a twenty-five percent commission on each one." Bingo! I was now in the transmission business.

Things were going nicely. The church pastor asked if Colleen and I would lead the Sunday school lesson for the youth. We agreed, and the next Sunday we started. After Sunday school and church was over, one of the other deacons came over to me and asked if I would do him a favor. His name was Joe. I said, "Sure, Joe, ask away."

He said, "I have been talking to John, who is in the Sunday school you and your wife are teaching. He has not made a commitment to accept Jesus as his personal savior. The favor is, would you meet me here at the church Saturday at five o'clock and pray with me one hour for John to accept Jesus and his gift of salvation?"

I replied, "Joe, it would be my pleasure to come and pray with you." So Saturday came. Four thirty came, and I told Colleen I was going to the church to pray with Joe for one half hour. Then I would be home for dinner. When I got to the church, Joe was just getting out of his car. He unlocked the side door of the church, and we both went to the altar and kneeled down and started to pray. We prayed for John. We both prayed out loud at different times, and when we both thought it was five thirty, we looked at the clock on the back wall. It was seven thirty. Neither one of us could believe we had prayed that long.

Sunday came, and we had Sunday school. John was there, and for the first time, he asked a couple of questions about salvation. Time was up. We prayed and were dismissed. I saw Joe in the hallway, waved to him, and he waved back. The service started. The choir sang. The preacher spoke. The service was ending when the preacher asked, "Is there anyone here who would like to accept the gift of salvation by accepting Jesus as their savior and following him in baptism?" John sent up to the altar, knelt down, and with teary eyes and sniffling noses, we both thanked God for our answered prayer.

Monday came, and it was back to work. We had a truck of batteries and supplies and oil, and three men and myself were just a little bit outside door of the office unloading the truck. Now I was licensed to carry a concealed weapon because of taking cash money to the bank. But while unloading the supplies from the truck, the boxes were hitting at my side right where the .38 revolver was on my hip. So I told the truck driver to hold on for a minute, and then I went over to my private office and removed the holster and gun from my hip. I locked the drawer and also locked the office door. I went back and started to unload the truck. A few minutes later I heard a scream from the front office. It sounded like my daughter Cindy. I ran into the office, and there was Cindy crying. The front pocket of her shirt was torn. She was holding her eye that had been injured, and Tammy was standing alongside Cindy. She was crying also. I yelled, "What's wrong?"

Tammy yelled, "Two men just robbed us and ran out the front door. One hit Cindy in her bad eye!"

I ran out from the front door and saw two men running toward the large vacant lot that was between our station and the Shell station. As I started running after the two men, I yelled to Colleen who was working the self service booth, "Call the police. Tell them we're being robbed now!"

I was not too far behind the two men when they split up. The one on the right side turned to the right and ran over a large dirt hill. The man that was on the left kept running straight. I yelled to the guy at the Shell who was standing there, "Stop him! He's a robber." As he made a move toward the robber, the robber stopped. When he did, I leaped on his back. I fell with him on the bottom and me on top of him with his face toward the ground. I pushed his face down into the dirt as hard as I could. He raised his head and said, "Stop, you're smothering me."

I told him, "You're lucky I don't kill you for what you did to my daughter." Again, his face kissed the dirt. The police officers came over. One who know me from coming in the station pulled me off the other guy. The second officer put his knee on the back of the suspect and put handcuffs on him.

I told the first officer, "I'll be right back. I have to see if my daughter is OK." I ran back over to the station. By that time the paramedics were there working on Cindy's eye. Tammy said the one that hit Cindy had said something about her eye just before he hit her. I took off running back across the field. I wanted to know if the one I caught was the one who hit Cindy. When I came around the back of the police car, the officers had the suspect standing against the car.

I screamed at him, "Are you the one who hit my daughter?"

He answered in very offensive way, "What if am?" what are you going to do about it?" I saw red, I mean real blood red. I shoved the police officer who was standing between the suspect and me, and the officer almost fell. I grabbed the suspect by the head and started smashing his head against the top of the police car. The officer who was holding the suspect let him go and tried to get me to stop pounding his head against the police car. The second officer got up off the ground, took a single handcuff out of his pocket, and while I pulled the bad guy's head forward, he put it on my right wrist and turned the top. It squeezed my wrist till I went down on my knees.

CHAPTER 11

The officers put him in the back seat of the car and took him away. The officers that were at the service station were still taking information from Cindy and Tammy. They asked me if I had any way of telling how much money had been taken. I told them I would not know until I checked out that night. So the officer said they would have a detective check with me next day. The paramedics said, "Her eye seems to be ok, but we want to take her to the hospital for further examination." So they took her to the hospital, and Colleen followed them in her car.

The next day the detective came around, and he and I went into my private office. Now that office was small. It had a desk, a chair, an adding machine, a curtain across the window in the front, and a safe on the floor, and the walls were covered with pictures of cowboy movie stars from the 1930s, '40s, and 50's. on the floor was a fifty-gallon barrel with a Western-style saddle strapped to it, and in front of it was a little horse-head stick. After talking for half an hour about my décor, he said, "We have identified the suspect. But I cannot reveal his identity to you. We need you to dome down to the station house tomorrow with your two daughters and your wife identify him in a lineup. I can tell you he worked for the post office." He left, and I made up my mind that when we were called down to the police station to identify him on the charges of robbery and assault, I was going to make sure he got what I felt he deserved.

By now the price of gasoline had gone up to one dollar and nine tenth of a cent. Amoco told us to set the price per gallon on the pump at half price, then if the customer asked for ten dollars, we were to put in five dollars and charge the customer ten dollars."

He said, "Yes, I asked you for ten dollars worth of gas, but you only gave me five dollars' worth."

I said, "No, sir, if you look at the price per gallon, you will see that it is half the price on the pump, which means we have to double the price per gallon."

He reached down under his leg and brought out a .45 automatic pistol, pointed it at me, and said, "What are you going to do if I don't pay?" I reached inside my jacket and pulled out of my belt a .22 pistol and stuck it just at his car window, which was open, and pointed it between his legs. "What are you going to do with that little thing?" he asked

I replied, "With that pistol you have, at this range, if you shoot me, chances are the bullet would go right through me. But if I get off a single shot from this little .22 and where I have it aimed, you won't die, but you sure won't be any good to anyone for the rest of your life."

He put his pistol on the seat next to him, reached in his jacket, took out a five-dollar bill, and hander me the two of them. As I took the money from him and backed away from the car, my pistol still in my hand and cocked. He said, "Don't ever expect to see me here ever again."

I replied, "Good. And happy motoring."

Colleen and I had to drive to Ocean City, Maryland, to a convention meeting of the Moose Lodge. on the way down, I saw a sign that read "Help wanted. Apply in person at Frontier Town." Directions were also written on the sign. I turned the cart where the sign was pointing, and she asked, "What are you doing?"

I told her, "I'm going to apply for a job."

She said, "You're crazy. They won't hire you."

I met the owner of Frontier Town and talked with him. "We'll," he said, "You take me by surprise asking about a job. Usually we hire all young high school kids while they are on summer vacation."

I said, "But wouldn't it be better to have an older person as sheriff or town marshal?"

He said, "You would have to bunk with the young people at night, you might not like the things they do."

I said. "That's not a problem. I have a mobile camper. I can drive here and rent a space in the campground at the back of the park for the summer."

He said, "I don't think I would have any outfits that would fit you."

I said, "Well, you can see by the way I dress that I have my own clothes."

"Well," he said, "I don't think we would have a holster that would fit you."

I said, "That's not a problem, I have a set of six shooters with pearl handles and a double holster set for them."

He said, "But you would have to buy your own blanks."

"That's OK," I said. "No problem."

He said, "Well, it looks like you really want the job, so I guess I'd better hire you. The job pays three dollars and fifty cents an hour. You get paid every Saturday after the last show. We won't be opening till the last week in June. We will be starting to get everything ready, but we will be painting, scrubbing, and cleaning equipment in May around the second week. I'll call you then to see if you still want the job."

I said, "Thank you, and you can bet your bottom dollar, if you call, I'll be here."

I went back to the car where Colleen was waiting, and as soon as I opened the car door, she said, "Don't tell me you got the job."

"Yes," I said, then we continued to the meeting at Ocean City.

April came and went. May came, and on the third week of May the phone rang. Colleen was in the collection booth and called over the speaker, "Hey, cowboy, it's Frontier Town calling."

I was so nervous. I said, "Hello."

He said, "Can you be here Monday?"

I said, "Yes."

He said, "See you then." And then he hung up. I was excited. I wanted to tell everyone. Now Colleen wasn't as excited as me about playing cowboys all summer. She said, "You can't go to Ocean City to pay cowboy and operate the service station from there. You have to make a choice." understood and said, "Why don't you go now, so you can be there before they come to check?"

I said, "I can't. I have to pay for the time I stayed at the camp site."

He said, "I also own the camp site. You don't owe anything. I hope you have a good luck at the service station."

I packed everything up, took an apple up the horse in the corral that I had been feeding every morning on my way to work, fired up the motor home, and headed back to Baltimore. I got back into the swing of things, and about a month later, the sales representative for Amoco came by with a very tempting sale offer. If I would purchase one hundred tires, they would take an additional 10 percent discount of the regular cost price. They would give me an extra ten tires free of charge. Also, they had the same special discount on batteries. If I bought fifty, they would give me five free. I took the deal. Colleen hit the ceiling. "We will never sell all those tires. We will sell the most popular ones and be stuck with the rest of the batteries. They'll all be dead before you sell ten." She ranted and raved at me for a week. Finally, I got tired of hearing about the tires and batteries. So I called another Amoco dealer who was on York Road not too far and not too close to where I was. I said to him, "How about if I sell a tire that I don't have in stock and you do, we make a trade on another size tire." He agreed, and we made the same deal on batteries. In three months, we were out of tires and batteries.

Now time had gone by, and Colleen had gone to the hospital for an operation. It was successful, but she needed some recovery time. Tammy had gotten her driver's license. I asked Ken if he could run the station without us for a week. He said, "Sure." So we packed up the motor home, and Colleen, Tammy, Cindy, Timmy, and me went off to California to visit Rudy and Hilda and take the kids to Disney World. We started out from the doctor's office. The doctor said Colleen could go but to take it easy. So off we went merrily on our way. I said to Colleen, "If you get sick on this trip, so help me, I will leave you where we are." We drove during the daylight hours and pulled into trailer parks in the early evening so the kids could enjoy the playground or the swimming pool. We finally arrived at the Disney World campsite. We checked in and went to visit Rudy and Hilda. We found their place, and because everybody was hungry, we decided to buy KFC fried chicken. We got a big bucket full and went back to Rudy and Hilda's apartment. It was late, and all the kids talked about was going to Disney World the next day. We drove back to the campsite pulled in and got everybody ready to sleep.

At about two thirty in the morning, I got the worst pain in my chest that I ever had. I got up put on my pants, and went outside the camper. I walked back and forth, trying to ease the pain. Finally, Colleen came out and asked what was wrong. I told her the pain in my chest was so strong that I could not even lie down to get rid of it. She said, "Get in. We're going to find a doctor or a hospital." We got back in the camper, and she rolled out. She drove up and down streets, stopping at every place that was open and looking for someone who knew where there was a hospital or a doctor's office. Finally a pair of flashing red lights flashed in our back window. It was a policeman telling us burned-out bulb in one of the blinker lights. Colleen said "I don't have time for that right now. Can you tell me where there is a doctor's office or a hospital?"

He said, "Make a left turn here, drive two blocks, turn right for four blocks, and you will find a doctor's office that is open twenty-four hours a day."

"Thank you," she said, and off we went. There was a nurse on duty at the table inside. I told her what was wrong, and she said, "I've got something here that will fix you right up." She gave me a shot something in my left arm. She said "This will take effect in about ten minutes. Go over to your camper, lie down, try to rest, and come back in half an hour."

I went out, laid in the camper, and rested.

"Come back in a half hour, and we'll see how you feel."

I did. When the half hour was up, I went back in, and the nurse asked how the pain was since she had given me the shot. I told her no better, maybe worse. She said, "Let me give you a stronger injection. I'll call an emergency doctor and see if we can get one over to check you out."

I laid on the table in another room. It was dark and quiet. What seemed like an hour went by, and then a man wearing a white doctor's coat came in and said, "I am Dr. Welby. I am going to examine you."

I could not resist the feeling. I had to ask, "Are you the real Dr. Welby, or are you an actor pretending to be Dr. Welby?"

He chuckled and said, "Ask me that question after you get my bill!"

I wanted to laugh, but it hurt too much. I woke up, and I thought it was morning because it was light outside. Colleen was sitting in a chair on the other side of the room. When she saw that I was awake, she buzzed for the nurse. The nurse came in, checked my vital signs, said I was doing OK, and then asked if I wanted dinner.

"Dinner?" I said, "No, I want breakfast."

She said, "I'm sorry, sir, we don't serve breakfast at four o'clock in the afternoon." She also said the doctor would be in in about twenty minutes and that he would be the one to set up a diet.

Colleen walked over and gave me a kiss and then said, "Remember what you said when we started out?"

I said, "No" (even though I did know).

She said, "You said if I got sick on this trip, you were going to leave me. Maybe you better think again the next time!"

We finally got home an unpacked. The next day when Colleen and I got to work, Ken said that the two men who were working at night were robbed at gunpoint last night and that the Amoco salesman was coming in today to talk to me. I did the paperwork and figured out that we lost six hundred dollars. I called the insurance company. They said they would be sending me out a form to fill out about the robbery and another form stating that they were cancelling our insurance coverage. Then the Amoco representative came in and said the company wanted me to keep the station open twenty-four hours, seven days a week, including all holidays. I had talked to Colleen about opening twenty-four hours, and she was against it. So I knew how she would feel. Called three other insurance companies but because of the previous robberies, the break-ins, and the amount for any vehicles kept overnight for service, their prices were too much. So I had no other choice but to try to sell the business to another dealer. I called a few other dealers I thought would be interested, and when I told them the price I wanted, they list interest.

Finally, after a few days, I got a call from another source asking if I was still interested in selling the business for forty thousand dollars. I said yes. He told me he would be over in two hours. He came, and I showed him around and told him what equipment came with the deal and also that the company wanted a twenty-four, seven-day-a-week lease. He agreed! He opened the briefcase he was carrying and said, "That's twenty thousand there. That's all I have right now, but I would be willing to pay you the other twenty thousand dollars in monthly payments every month."

I called my account met and asked his advice. He said, "You're getting what you wanted. Take the deal. But tell him you want 7 percent interest per month on the remaining balance."

The buyer agreed, I said, "When would you want to take over?"

He said, "Tomorrow morning."

I called my account again and asked if he could have a contract of sale drawn up by tomorrow morning at 7:00 a.m. He said he could. So the next morning at 7:00 a.m., we changed hands. We signed the contracts. He gave me the briefcase. The deal was done.

I gathered my employees in the front office, told them what had just happened, and gave each one of them their week's pay, and as a thank you for their service, and extra week's pay. After we left the office, I heard the new dealer offer jobs to anyone who wanted to stay on. I told Ken to hold off getting another job as Ken's bonus. We were taking them to Las Vegas for a week at our expense except for gambling money. (Remember the two tickets from our Chicago stayover? We used them to pay their airfare.) after we all came back from Vegas, Colleen asked what we were going to do with the money we had left. I said, "Put it in the bank until we need it."

She said, "I want a thousand dollars."

"What for?" I asked.

She said, "You had your own service station. I want to open my own business."

I said, "OK, but what kind of business are you going into?"

She said, "There is a lady who was a Christian bookstore at the mall on Harford Road. She told me that she has another store that is closed over on Eastern Avenue. She said that she would rent me by the month and that I could open a store there."

"OK," I said. "Half the money we have is yours anyway. So if you want to use it to open a Christian bookstore, that's OK with me. But let's go take a look at it first."

The next day we rode over to Eastern Avenue. The store was the fourth in a row of seven stores. There was no parking lot close by.

CHAPTER 12

The area had parking meters that you had to pay to park at. I told her that the location was not good for what she wanted to do. She did not want to listen and went and paid the lady a month's rent. There were two rooms and a bath on the second floor, and behind the room that would be used for the showroom, there was another room with a small kitchen behind it. So I asked her if she wanted me to help her clean it out and get her set for her grand opening. She said, "Yes, but after that I make all the decisions about the business. You keep out of it!"

Well, it was obvious she did not want any help. So I let her tell me what she wanted downstairs and what she wanted upstairs. She finally got ready to open, but first she found something I had fixed for her that she didn't ask for. Under the steps that led up to the second floor I had hung a curtain to block the opening under the steps. Inside I had put a chair with an opening in the center with a large metal barrel under it and a small table with two rolls of toilet paper on it. She said, "What's that?"

I said, "You 're going to be here from eight a.m. to at least six p.m. every day, all day. I think that may come in handy."

She didn't like it because she didn't think about it, but over the next few months, it served its purpose. Over the next two weeks, I stayed busy, looking around the neighborhood for work that I could do. Having no success, I started to read the want ads in the newspaper. I saw an ad by Montgomery Ward- "Appliance salesman wanted. Apply on person"- with the location of the store. Colleen had her own car. And I had the four-wheel drive with a snowplow on the front that we had used for road service at the station. I drove to Montgomery Ward and got a job. It paid commission only on whatever you sold. The manager told me he would put someone with me for the first week, then I would be on my own.

The first week went by. I had listened to the man who was teaching me how he greeted customers, introduced himself, and closed the sale. The next week I greeted my first customer on my own, helped her with her selection, and closed the deal. *Great, I made my first commission*, I thought. Later I greeted another customer, helped her to decide what color curtains she wanted, and before I could close the sale, the other salesman came over and said, "I worked with this lady last week, and she just came in today to close the sale from last week. So she is my customer." I went to the manager and told him my complaint. He said, "Fred's right. That was his customer. He gets the commission." I asked how long Fred had been employed there."

He said, "Two years, and he has done an outstanding job!"

I said, "That's great. But I can't work nothing, so I quit!"

The manager said, "Wait, wait, don't be hasty. You worked in automotive. How would you like to have the job of shop manager? That pays a salary of two hundred dollars a week plus 5 percent of all sales." Well, the salary wasn't that great, but I could do good on the commission. So I agreed. They only paid every two weeks, so I had to work three weeks without a paycheck. Meanwhile people were bringing their cars in every day, and I was writing orders, hand over fist, and keeping the three technicians busy. Payday rolled around. I got my paycheck and almost passed out when I saw the total. I had made my salary less than the state and federal taxes, and where it said "Percent of commission," it said zero. I went again to see the manager, and after showing him copies of the jobs I had written, he said, "How many of those jobs did you actually do?"

I said, "None. I was hired to write orders and pass them out to the techs."

"That's right," said the manager. "But we expect you to do some work too. You are supposed to do jobs, and that's what you get paid commission on."

I said, "I'm going to lunch." I got in my car and left.

A few days later I saw an ad: "Assistant Manager trainees needed. Apply at Roy Rogers restaurants." I thought, *Boy! This would be great*. So I dressed in my finest Wester wear-boots, hat, the whole nine yards. I walked into Roy Rogers restaurant and asked for the manager. He came around the corner from the kitchen, turned, pushed open the door to the kitchen, and said, "Jeff! You got to see this!" Jeff came out, took one look at me, looked over at the manager, looked back at me, and said, "Are you Roy Rogers?"

I said, "Well, howdy, partner. No, I'm Roy, but I am looking for job."

He said, "Wait right here." He left, came back in about five minutes, and said, "Would you mind taking a ride with me? There's someone who wants to see you."

I said. "OK."

We got in his car and drove to a Marriot Hotel. We got out of the car and walked into the lobby. Eyes were looking at me. Some little kids come over. I shook hands and said, Howdy, little buckaroos."

Jeff said, "Come this way." We walked behind the desk into another area where another man was sitting. He looked up, dropped his pen that he was writing with, and said to Jeff, "Your right. I know it's not him, but there is a close resemblance!"

He asked for my name. I told him, and we talked. That was Mr. Marriot, and the next day I was an employee of Roy Rogers Inc. I was assigned to a restaurant and told, "Don't wear uniform. Wear your regular clothes, and when they get dirty, you get them cleaned and bring us the bill."

Now because I was being trained as an assistant manager, I had to work most nights. The restaurant was closed at eleven, but by the time we got everything cleaned up and put away, it was after twelve thirty, and I had about an hour's drive from work to home.

Meanwhile, Colleen was not doing well with her Christian bookstore. She could not even make the rent. So, finally, after three months, she gave up. She sent back whatever inventory she could and sold what she could at or below cost just to get rid of them. I spent some time going to the other dealers I knew, but nobody said anything about working for them. I was getting pretty discouraged. Meanwhile, Colleen talked to the preacher's wife about her job. Colleen was very interested and put in an application. About three weeks went by, and then she got the job of a lifetime for her. She was hired as an air courier. Her job was to be at the airfield one hour before the plane was to take off. The armored truck would bring cash, food stamps, bonds, and anything that had to be shipped overseas. She would be stationed at the cargo hole in the plane. The armored truck would arrive, unload whatever was to be shipped, and she would have to stand there until all the other cargo was loaded. The cargo door was shut and locked, and then she had to stand nearby until all the passengers were onboard. She would always be the last one to get aboard the aircraft and the first one to get off the plane when it landed so she could be at the cargo door before it was opened.

Meanwhile, I had talked to Rudy by phone, and he was encouraging me to come to California to work and to live. Finally, after the dealer who bought the service station from us paid off the other twenty thousand dollars plus interest, there wasn't much less. Colleen agreed for me to go to California to go to work. But she made some stipulations that she thought were impossible to obtain. She said, "If you fly to California, you must work all day, light hours, no nights. You must be off on Saturdays and Sundays, and you have to do it in three months. If you get all that then in October, I'll move out there with you."

I said, "OK, it's a deal." I remember reading in the Bible the verse that says "nothing is impossible if you put your faith in God." So I flew to Costa Mesa, California. It had been raining there for three days before I arrived. I landed, got off the plane, got my luggage, and walked out the front door of the airport. I looked to my left and saw a statue that looked to be ten feet tall.

I had landed at John Wayne Airport. I thought to myself, *This must be a good sign.* Rudy met me there, and we drove to his place. Remember back near the beginning of this book when I told you what a good mechanic Rudy was? Well, what I'm going to tell you next, you may not want to believe. Now when we had come to visit Hilda and Rudy last time, they were living in an apartment. Well, they bought a piece of property and built a wooden fence ten feet high on three sides. At the front entrance was an eight-foot wire fence with a double wide on it. Rudy had built that with only Hilda helping him. He had bought a Ford pickup truck, removed the back from the frame, lengthened the frame, and made a camper out of it. The camper was just perfect for two people, as I found out later. It had a couch that opened into two beds and could be folded up to be a couch the three people could sit on comfortably. A table was anchored to the floor but could easily be removed if you just wanted to sit and talk, or it could be easily put back in place when it was time to eat. There was a stove, a double sink, and a bathroom with a shower and commode. Over the front he had made and welded to the roof another size big enough for two adults. He had also, at some time, purchased a used school bus. He had made metal pieces to cover some of the windows on the outside and to use as paneling for the inside, covering from floor to roof. There was a two-bed bedroom across the back with a built in vanity and cloth closet. There was a kitchen with a stove and a sink, a living room with TV, and of course, a rebuilt engine. I was amazed. I told him I had to go get a room. "Non-sense," Hilda said." We've got plenty of room here. You put your belongings in the camper we got there, and you eat your meals here with us."

So I was all set. California, here I come. I plugged the camper into the electric outlet and, presto, lights, TV, air Conditioning. I slept like a baby that night. The next day after breakfast, Rudy took me to a couple of shops where he thought I might get hired on. No luck. One week went by. Rudy came out of the camper one night and said, "You ought to be able to find your way around here by now. So here." He handed me a key.

"What's this?" I asked.

He said, "It's the ignition key for the Volkswagen out there. You can use it while you're here."

I said, "But you don't have to do all this."

He said, "I talked you into coming out here. The least I can do is help you get around."

Well, another two weeks went by, and to be perfectly honest, I was beginning to doubt. I had worked as a gas station in Maryland in a place called Little Italy for about a year. And when I told the manager I was moving to California, he had tried to talk me into staying. So when my notice was up, he said, "Anytime you want to come back, you got a job here." I said to myself, "OK, two more days, and I'm going back to Baltimore."

The next day I was looking through the paper, and an ad caught my eye. "Service station manager wanted. Apply at Fitzgerald's Amoco," and it gave the location. I asked Rudy how to get there, and he told me, "That's in Costa Mesa." So he gave me directions, I found the station. It was doing a great business. There were three sets of gas pumps outside and lifts with cars on all of them. I asked for the manager. "He's not here, but his wife is here. Would you like to talk to her?" the serviceman asked.

I said, "Yes please."

He went, and she came over to where I was standing and asked if she could be of assistance. I said, "I would like to apply for the manager's job."

She said, "My husband usually does all the hiring, but if you would like to fill out an application, I will see that he gets it."

I said, "OK, thank you." I filled out the application and handed it to her.

She looked at it and said, "You haven't been in California long, have you?"

I replied, "No, ma'am, I just moved here."

She said, "How long do you intend to live here?"

I said without thinking, "As long as God Almighty wants me to stay."

She said, "Good!"

The next afternoon Hilda told me, "While you were out, a man called and said he wanted to talk to you about a job. He left his number and said to tell you don't take any job until you speak to him." I called the number. It was Fitzgerald's Amoco. I asked to talk to Mr. Fitzgerald, and after a small while, he came to the phone. I told him who I was and that he said I should call him before taking any other job.

He said, "Yes, I am looking for someone to manage my other location. It is over on the outskirts of Corona Del Mar. are you familiar with the area?"

I said, "No, sir, I am not. I've only been here a little over a week, and I'm still finding my way around."

He said, "Meet me tomorrow morning at this location at nine a.m. You do know how to get here, don't you?"

I said, "Yes, sir, I do. I've been there before."

"OK, I'll see you in the morning."

I got up the next morning. Hilda fixed me breakfast and insisted that I eat before left because I did not know what time I would get back. I got to his location at about eight thirty. He was surprised that I was that early. We got in his pickup truck and drove to his other location. It was a beautiful location. It was on an open highway that could handle four lanes of traffic. Across from the station was the Pacific Ocean. There were large palm trees planted on both sides of the highway. The station itself sat back a way from the road. There was an office, two service bays, and two sets of gas pumps out front with automatic fill handles. There were two men working there when we pulled up. We got out of the truck, went inside the service bay, and he introduced me to Gus (he was the mechanic) and the other was Phil. He said that Phil had been running the station but was going to go back to school in two weeks, and that was why he needed a manager. Gus count not handle the mechanical work and manage too. He said that after school started, Phil would be coming in on Saturdays and Sundays. If I took the job, those would be my days off. He asked me what I thought.

I said, "Well, we have not talked about salary, hours, or how much they are and what I would have over the employees."

He said I would be expected to work forty hour a week and that my salary would be five hundred dollars paid weekly on Friday at about three o'clock. "if for any reason, you have to work forty hours, you get paid time and one half. I will also give you a two weeks vacation with pay after one year and a five-thousand-dollar insurance policy that we pay for. How does that sound?"

I said, "I think you just hired yourself a manager." I started to work the next morning. I opened up at 7:00 a.m. Gus came in at eight. Customers were coming in and filling up, and I would ask if they would like me to check under the hood.

Things worked along good, and I called Colleen and said, "Guess what? I got the job with everything you wanted plus a little bit more. When will you be coming out? I miss you."

"Well," she said, "I have to give two weeks notice, have to find some place to store our furniture, and have to get a school certificate to change the kids' school, so it will probably be another four to five weeks."

I said, "OK, but make it as quick as you can."

Two weeks after that, I came home after work, and Hilda said, "We're going to eat out tonight. So you go out to the camper, get cleaned up, and change your clothes, then we will go eat." I went out to the camper, opened the door, and heard a word. The word was *hi*. It was Colleen! She had gotten everything done, caught a late flight, and came to surprise me. I hugged her and kissed her and held her.

A week later I took Colleen and the kids up to MGM Studios on a tour. The kids were always running ahead of us. It was kind of a hot and sticky Saturday. We took the kids into the cafeteria and ordered them each an ice-cream sundae. When I turned to go to the table where Colleen and

I were sitting, a short man in a cowboy outfit went by me. I turned and in a loud voice, said, "Hi, Little Texas!"

He stopped, turned to me, and said, "It's been a long time since anyone has called me that!" sure enough, I was right. It was Audie Murphy, the most decorated hero of World War Two. We shook hands, and I said, "I'm sorry about your wound."

He said, "That's OK. Had it not been for getting wounded, I would have stayed in the army. But God has a way turning bad things into good results. Gotta go, thanks for remembering." And he left. We would go up to Hollywood or to swim in the Pacific Ocean almost every weekend.

One day Mr. Fitzgerald met me at the station before opening time. I knew something was wrong, but I didn't know what. When I went in and said "good morning." He said, "I told you when I hired you that nobody got credit. Everything was cash or credit card, and yet you gave this old lady one hundred dollars credit for an alternator. Why?"

"Well, she needs her car for work. She comes in at least twice a week to fill her tank with fuel, and I didn't think you would mind. After all, you did make me manager."

He said, "I should fire you!"

I said, "Don't bother. I quit." I spent about two weeks looking for work, and one day, there was an ad in the paper. Jiffy Lube was hiring manager trainees. I applied, was selected, and started manager training. Two weeks later I took a final test and passed. So I was told I would be manager of the shop in Costa Mesa, a small but growing area right at the back part of the John Wayne Airport. I had three men working with me. One worked in the lower bey (under the car), the second worked the upper bay (under the hood), and the third man did cursory washing of the outside of the windows, vacuuming the front and rear seat areas, and checking the setting of the tire pressure. My job was to greet the customer and explain to him or her what we did and long it would take and what it would cost. It went like this, "Good morning, sir or ma'am, have you ever been to Jiffy Lube before? No? Well, let me tell you what we will do. We will change your oil, draining the old oil out of your vehicle and adding up to five quarts of proper grade engine oil. We will also lubricate the car chassis and check and top off your differential. We also check and top off your transmission, check your air filter, and check and top off your radiator and brake fluid.

We check your windshield wipers, vacuum your car's interior, and inflate your tire pressure to normal. We do all this ten minutes or less, and the is only 19.95. would you like our full service today? Thank you." I worked for Jiffy Lube for three years.

Meanwhile, Ken and Pat and their two children moved to California, they were across town from us but still close enough to visit every once in a while. I talked Ken into going to Jiffy Lube, and he did. He was hired as a store manager but really wasn't happy. He later transferred to merchandising for Jiffy Lube leases. Later Jiffy Lube franchised out all their shops and anyone who was managing had two sons that he put in charge. I was still making manager's wages, so it wasn't too bad. At least, I didn't have to do paperwork.

One day I was working on a customer's vehicle. I was checking his air filter when I put my hand in to removing the filter. A critter hissed at me and tried to bite my hand. It turned out to be a possum, and it scared me more than I scared him. The next day I had off, I went to a shop that did the same type of service but was not Jiffy Lube. He said he could use me as an upper bay technician. I agreed to start the next day. I went back to Jiffy Lube and quit. I also started to serve morning and Sunday newspapers. Sometimes the papers would be late at my drop-off area, and by the time I finished delivering them, I was late for work.

Now Colleen had not been happy living in California, so she talked me into moving back to Baltimore. Ken, Pat, and their two sons were ready to move back also. So we purchased a station wagon, and we loaded everything we could load in there. We had a cat, and she rode on top of all our stuff from California to Baltimore. Ken rented a large truck, and we loaded both of our house hold furniture and tv into the truck. It was full from top to bottom and from front to back. I had gone back to Jiffy Lube's main office to say goodbye to the man who hired me. He said, "What are you going to do when you go back?"

"I'll find a job doing something. I don't know what."

He said, "Here's the name and phone number of a dealer that has three shops in Baltimore. He may be able use you. Give him a call"

I said, "Thanks for everything." We shook hands, and then I got in the car and left. The next day we all got up at 5:00 a.m. Colleen and I had the three kids in the seat of the station wagon followed by Ken in the big truck with Richard, Pat, and shawn in their car and bringing up the rear. We drove all that day, and when we stopped, we found a motel that had a swimming pool and a workout room. We all spent the night at the motel and then got up early for the next day of our journey. We traveled that second day, stopping only for bathroom breaks, drinks and food and fuel so we wouldn't have to waste too much time. We didn't waste too much time, but we didn't rush either. One stop we did make was in Missouri where we played the machines for about an hour and won more that we lost. The whole trip took us six days.

When we got home we had to spend another two days finding places to live. Pat and Ken found a house they could rent that was close to where Pat's parents lived. Colleen, the kids, and myself found a house that for rent with tie option to buy. We moved in. Now our children were old enough to take care of themselves. I went to see the owner of the Jiffy Lube shops. He gave me a job right away but said he wanted me to work at a store with another manager so he could what I knew before he gave me a shop to operate. Two weeks went by. then the owner came in and said, "OK, Wes, I'm ready to turn the shop over to you. Come get in my car, and I'll take you there just look around and sort of get acquainted."

He drove to near where Pimlico Raceway is located. Two blocks away on the west side was the shop. He parked on the side, and we walked into the office. The ashier looked up, smiled, and said, she was glad to see him. He introduced me and said I was going to be the new manager, then we went down into the lower bay, and it was a mess. Inventory that had been dropped off was still In boxes. The windshield washer was extremely low in the barrel, and grease guns were just that. He then took me back upstairs and showed me the car wash machine on the side of the shop. He asked me how long it would it take to get the shop in shape.

I said, "How many people do I have here to work with?"

He said, "Five. This is a four-bay shop. You have five workers plus a car wash on the outside. You are open from eight a.m. to six p.m. That's ten hours a day, six days a week."

"We are going to need at least six personnel."

He said, "OK, I'll put an ad in the paper tomorrow and run it for a week. I'll have them report to you here, and you can handpick the ones you need."

"Sounds like a good deal," I said. we drove back to his office, and he gave me a set of keys and said, "I just had the locks changed on the box at the wash and on the front door."

I said, "Good."

He handed me a whole bunch of papers. "Those are employment applications. Use as many as you need. Get some for when you have to ire new employees."

"OK," I said. I was all set. The next morning, I went to the shop early and let myself in. I sat down at the desk and waited. The cashier was the first one to the door. It was seven fifty. I unlocked the door, bid her good morning, and she started to count her cash till. At ten after two team members came in. one went down to lower bay, and the other one went into the lounge and sat down and started to pick up the newspaper and read it. I asked the cashier what time the rest of the crew came in. she said, "This is all that comes in until after school lets out." The phone rang. I answered it. It was someone who read the help wanted ad in the newspaper. I told him I would be there all day, and I felt sure there would a space for him. A customer pulled up to the door and beeped his horn. The employee reading the paper kept on reading. The cashier went to the bay door and opened it and said, "You here for an oil change?" The customer said yes.

"OK, leave your keys in the ignition, and I'll have somebody pull your car in," she replied. Then she yelled to the tech sitting in the lounge, "Hey, Albert, you got a customer."

"OK," Albert replied. "I'll be there in a couple of minutes."

I had heard enough. I walked into the lounge. The customer was seated there. I said, "Albert, I need you out here now!"

He said, "OK boss." He came out. I was ready to rip him apart. But I knew that would only make a bad situation worse. So I said as firm as I could without yelling. "Get that hood open, and get started now! And use the proper commands so the customer knows he gets what he pays for!"

Then I went down to lower bay and talked to the person there.

"What is your name?" I asked.

"Steve," he replied.

"Well, Steve we are going to have a meeting after we close tonight, but right now I want you to do your job and make sure to use proper commands while you do your job." I went back upstairs, took two paper towels and a half-empty spray, and started washing the windows and inspecting the windshields wipers. They were both torn on the edges and lying flat on the windshield. I told Albert as I removed the wipers, "When you go into the lounge to make your sales presentation, sell him a new set of wiper blades." I then turned on the vacuum cleaner and vacuumed the front and rear carpet and floor mats. Then I used the tire machine to check and set his tire pressure at the proper level. We finished the service, and Albert went to start the car. I stopped him and said, "Do the safety check."

He said, "What's that?"

I called, "Safety check, lower bay."

Steve called back "hand on the differential plug. Plug tight. Hand on oil. Plug tight and dry. Hand on oil filter. Filter hot and tight. Safety check complete, bay 1."

I called a meeting that evening and told that we were going to have thirteen workers in the shop and it was going to be run by the book. I also hired a second cashier. So now I had a full crew. Albert, Tim, and Sam were my upper bay people. Steve, John, Don were my lower bay people. Harry and George were my courtesy people. Alice and Mary were my cashiers. They each received individual training by me.

Business was improving. The shop was looking cleaner and brighter, and the car wash was making a lot more money. I had now worked there a little more than a year. Everyone was working by the book until on Saturday before Christmas. I told all the help, "When you go to pull a car over the bay, always make sure there is someone standing at the front of the pit. When you start to pull a car over the pit, the person at the front of the car should guide you in safely and will use arm signals. And to make sure there is no one in the lower bay in harm's way, that person should shout "car coming in bay 2 or 1 or 3 or 4." But always make sure there is someone to guide you in." That Saturday before Christmas after work the boss was throwing a Christmas party for both of the locations. It was to start at seven thirty. Colleen had driven me to work that day and was bringing me clean clothes to wear at the party. We were also going to get our Christmas bonus checks.

I guess one of the guys got a little excited about the party and decided to bring a vehicle in with out a guide. Well, he had just gotten the motor part over the pit when he moved the steering wheel, and the front end of the car went down in the pit. There we were, standing there and trying to figure out how to get the car out of the pit. we finally decided to call a towing company. The hood and grill were damaged, and the right front part of the fender was torn away from the frame. The car could not be driven, and the front passenger side door would not open. The tow truck finally came and pulled the car out. I asked if his company could fix the damage. He said sure but that because of the Christmas holiday, the shop has closed early. He said, "I can put in on the side of your shop and come back Monday and tow it in and give you an estimate on the repair parts."

I said, "OK, go ahead." He did, then he left. We all pitched in to get cleaned up to go to the party. The cashiers were figuring out from the tickets how much business we had done that day, then adding up the money and credit cards to make sure they matched. And then they would put the money and checks in a locked bag so I could take it to the night deposit at the bank. I said to Allice, "While you're doing that, I'm going around the side of the building to make sure that the damaged car is locked. I went around the side. By this time it was dark, even darker than usual with all the lights from the shop being off. I pulled on the driver's side door, and it was open. I got in between the front seats and leaned over to check the two back doors. They were locked. I tried the passenger side front door, and it was locked. I started to back out, bent over and sort of crawling backward out the door.

Just then l left something hard hit the back of my head. I fell forward over the front seat and was able to turn while I was falling, so now I was on my back looking up at two men wearing hood masks. The closest to the steering wheel was holding a long metal pipe in his hand. He kept swinging it at me, but because of the steering wheel, he could not get a good swing. The second man was busy pulling at my shirt pockets, and when he tried to get into my side pants pocket, I was able to grab his hand and twist it. He pulled back, came another step closer to the car, and tried to get my wallet out of my left rear pocket. When he moved, he gave me just enough room that I could get my left leg up. I pulled my leg up and was able to give him a hard kick in a place he would remember for a long time. The other fellow had pulled the pipe out and pushed it in under the steering wheel. I was able to grab the end of the pipe, and instead of pulling it in to me, I shoved it into his stomach just as hard as I could. At that time a dark-colored car pulled up behind them, and I heard a voice say, "Come on. You're taking too long." They got into the car, taking their pipe with them. I got out of the car just in time to see the shadow of the dark car turn the corner on the right with no lights on, so I could not see a license plate.

I staggered around the corner of the building hollering, "Help, help." No one heard me, and as I stumbled through the back door, Alice screamed and told someone to get a towel and some water. She also yelled for someone to call for an ambulance and to call the police. The police arrived first, and I told them what had happened. While I was telling the first officer what took place, the second officer went to the police car and got out a first aid kit and tried to stop some of the bleeding. The ambulance came. The EMS guys came in, and as soon as one looked at my head, he said, "You got to go to the hospital. Can you walk, or do you want a stretcher?"

I said, "No, I can walk." I also said to Alice, "My wife is supposed to picked me up here to go to the Christmas party. Tell her what happened and to meet me at the hospital."

They put me in the back of the ambulance. One of the men got in with me and said, "It's better if you sit up and let me hold this towel on your head to help stop the bleeding." So off we went to the hospital. When we got me there, they walked me inside, and the nurse said, "What do we have here

They EMS man said, "This guy was beaten up, and I think he is going to need stitches."

So they took me to an emergency room. The doctor came in and told a nurse, "Clean the wound, cut hair from area, and stop the bleeding." The doctor had just finished putting seventeen stitches when my wife arrived and came right into the room. "What happened?" she asked, and I told the doctor and her what had happened.

The doctor looked at my wife and said, "Mrs. Watts, it's a good thing God gave your husband a hard head or he would be not be walking out of this hospital." He also said to her, "He may have a headache for one or two days. It's normal. Just give him aspirin every four to five hours till the pain goes away."

They released me, and Colleen said to me, "Well, you've certainly had an exciting night. I guess your ready to go home?"

I said, "No way. Were going back to the shop to pick up the money bag and take it to the bank. Then we're going to the Christmas party." She looked at me in disbelief.

We got to the Christmas party. Festivities were still going on. We opened the door, and when I entered the room, everybody started to clap. The boss stood by the table where I had sat down. I was getting a little wobbly. He said, "Wes, I have already given out the Christmas bonus and made my speech, but I just want to say to you, you did more than what anybody would have expected. Here's your Christmas bonus, along with my thanks." I thanked him.

He said, "How long did the doctor say you would be off?"

Now the whole top of my head was covered with bandages, and my shirt still had drying bloodstains when I said, "I'll be in on Monday."

Colleen said, "No, you won't. you're going to need a least two weeks off."

The boss said, "She's right, at least two weeks, and it will be with pay." We left the party, and Colleen drove home.

The next day was Sunday. I got up, got dressed and got ready to go to church. Colleen asked me if I thought I would be able to sit through the service without having to get up and leave while the service was going on. I said, "I'll be OK. God didn't bring me through all this for me to lie in bed on his holy day. Yes, if God stands with us, who can stand against us?"

By the time church was over and I had told the story of what happened, I was feeling the pain. So we went home, and I went to bed. I slept off and on, and on Monday morning I was glad that Colleen and my boss had told me to take the week off. Later on that day the boss called the house and told Colleen to tell me that he talked to the doctor and that the doctor wanted me off for at least three weeks. When the time was up, I went to the office and talked to the employer. He asked how I felt about carrying a firearm at work. I told him I had a .38 six-shot pistol at home from when I had the service station. He said, "Good. Start carrying it. I'll get you a permit." He also said, "Because you are going to be gone longer than anyone planned, I hired an assistant manager to help you with your duties. We are also opening the car wash on Sundays, and he will be there from eight a.m. until four p.m."

So I returned to work. But things were not the same as before the assault. So I decided to look for another source of income. A man I knew asked me if I know anyone looking for work. I said yes. He said, "I would like to talk to him."

I said, "You are."

He said, "You? You? You don't know anything about running a lamp manufacturing plant."

I said, "Yes, you're right. I don't know anything about assembling lamps, but the people that work there do. And while I am keeping them busy for you, I can be learning from them."

He said, "That's pretty good. I never thought of it like that. OK, you're hired. When can you start?"

I said, "I'll be at your shop Monday morning at eight a.m."

He met me there, and there God did it again. When he closes one door, he opens another.

CHAPTER 13

Now the lamp-making business isn't really that complicated. As a lamp manager I had to make sure that we had enough glassware for all orders. All orders came into the office to one of two secretaries and order fillers. The boss also worked in that office. When the orders came in, the customer was told it would take two weeks to make the lamps. Then they would fax the order to me. I would check through our stock of clear lamp styles. The orders were listed as quantity, size, shape, color, base, outlet, then underneath that was listed shade = color, size, shape, final, to be delivered at day / date / time. Then my job began to get tedious. I had to make sure we had enough clear glass on hand to fill the order. This was the job of the stock boy. Then the clear glass was given to the painter. He would paint the glass on the inside. Then after the paint was dry, the lamps went to the assembly tables. There were two men that worked that area, and I was supposed to learn how to put them together just to keep me busy. They would get the base (wood or brass) the height pole that went from the bottom through the top. After that it was the electric wiring, either brown, black, or white. Then it was the little thing that screws on top to hold the lamp together. Then we would put them in boxes and load them on the delivery truck, and the deliveryman would take them to the shade assembly plant that was three blocks away.

Now the owner always called the manager' meeting on Friday mornings. He would provide coffee and doughnuts. And as soon as he, both secretaries, the shade plant manager, and me were all there, he would always open with the same question: what have you brought to the table today? Boy, did I get tired of that. Finally, one Friday I stopped at Krispy Kreme on my way to work, bought two dozen mixed doughnuts, took one dozen over to lamp shop for my crew, and held the other dozen for the meeting. When it was time for the meeting, I put the box of doughnuts on the floor under my chair. No one knew it was there except me. First to arrive after me was Amanda. She was a very pretty woman, very sweet, and always ready to help me with any problem I had. She always came over at lunchtime to have lunch in my office with me. This one particular Friday, the boss, as usual, was the last one to come in to the meeting. He sat down and said, "Good morning, everyone." Then he started around the table asking the same tired question. "What do you bring to the table today?"

When he came to me, I made a big thing of it. I said, "Today I have brought to this table something that we all can enjoy and take part in. "I reached under the chair and sat the box of Krispy Kremes on the table. Everyone laughed out loud, and even the boss chuckled a bit. After the meeting was over, we all went to our different areas. At about eleven fifteen I got a call from Amanda. She said, "Wes, the boss wants to talk to you in your office at eleven forty-five."

"OK, thank you," I said and hung up. When he came in, I was sitting at the desk looking over some future orders. He sat down and said, "That was a pretty funny stunt you pulled this morning, but I didn't hire you for your sense of humor. So let's not have any more of it."

I said, sarcastically, "OK, boss," and he left.

A few minutes later the phone rang. It was Amanda. She said, "The boss just left. Do you still have a job?"

I said, "Yes, he read me the riot act about my sense of humor and told me to stop."

She said, "I'm glad he didn't fire you! Are we going to have lunch together?"

I said, "We always do, don't we?"

She said, "OK, see you then," and hung up. Lunch time came. We sat in my office to eat. The crew had gone out to lunch, so the was empty. After we finished eating, said, "I have worked here, but I have never seen how this part of the plant operates. We have some time left. How about giving me tour?"

I said, "Sure, come on." We walked out of the office.

Saturday came and Colleen and I went shopping as we usually did, we went to church service on Sunday and to Sunday school. I felt strange and uncomfortable all during the service. Even to the point of thinking to myself, *How does the preacher know what happened?* I thought about what happened and made up my mind that Satan was not going to get my soul.

Monday came around, and I went to work. I got there early, hoping that Amanda would call and that I could tell her it was over. She did not call or come over for lunch. The day came to an end. So I locked everything and drove home. The next day, Tuesday, was +my birthday. I got up, got dressed as usual, and ate breakfast. Colleen said, "Honey, I'm taking you out for dinner tonight at the steak house. So don't be late."

I said, "OK, I won't." I got to work and started to get some orders together. The crew started to show up. I was determined to tell Amanda it was over. Lunchtime came, and the crew had not gone out to lunch like they always did. The front doorbell rang. One of the guys opened the door and walked Amanda carrying a large box and a small box. It was both the girls from the office and the seven workers and shop manager from the shade plant. I walked out of the office to see what was going on. they all shouted, "Happy birthday!" they all sang "Happy Birthday to you." I was shocked. I did not think anything like this was going to happen. Amanda came over to me and handed me the small box she was holding and said, "Happy Birthday, Wes. This little token of appreciation is for you from all of us." I opened it up, and inside was large coffee cup. Inscribed on the cup was a saying that read "On your birthday there where a million people born. This makes you one in a million! Happy birthday." She cut the cake, and we all shared it till it was all gone. Then lunch time was coming to a close, I stood up and said, "I want to thank each and every one of you for sharing your lunch hour with me. It makes me feel like I am really welcome here and really wanted. Thank you all!"

the ladies from the shade shop started leaving, and as each one left, the kissed me on the cheek and said "happy birthday." The men who worked in the shop shook my hands and said "happy birthday." The two office people were last to leave. The first girl gave me a kiss on the cheek and said "happy birthday" and left. What was wrong with me? Why couldn't I stop? I prayed as hard as I could, asking God, "What shall I do?"

on Thursday he gave me the answer-"move on." I asked, "What do you mean, God, by move on? how can I move on when we both work in so contact?" Again, I heard "move on." Friday morning came, and we all got ready for your weekly meeting. I had Stopped at the Texaco station on the corner and talked to Len. He was the one who gave me such a great reference when I was in California. I told him I needed a job. He said, "When can you start?"

I said, "This afternoon."

He said, "Wait till Monday, and I'll see you here ready to work at seven a.m."

I said, "Thanks. See you Monday." I went back to the glass shop, straightened out the orders, and put all the orders in order. I went to the office and waited for the boss. I had written my resignation out on Thursday at home and had it all ready for Friday's meeting. When the boss came in, he sat down and started in his usual way. "What have you brought to the table today?" Before anyone could say anything, I threw my letter on the table. He picked it up, opened it, and read it. He said, "Are you sure this is what you want to do? And how you want to do it?"

I said, "Yes, sir, I am sure."

He said, "OK, if that's what you want, I see no need for you to stay for this meeting." I got up and walked out. That was done. What a relief. There was just one more thing to be settled. What about Amanda? How could I explain this to her? She came out the front door. I grabbed her arm and said, "Amanda, we have got to talk!"

She said, "Yes, we sure do."

I said, "Not here, not now."

She said, "Then where and when? I have to know!"

I said, "Tonight at five o'clock I'll meet you at the seafood restaurant over at the inner harbor."

She said, "OK, but please be there. Don't leave me hanging in suspense!"

That was the longest afternoon I had ever spent, just waiting for five o'clock to come. I got to the restaurant at four thirty, sat down at a table, and told the waiter to bring me a drink. When he brought my drink, I told him I was expecting to meet a lady friend there at five o'clock. He said he would keep an eye out for her and bring her over as soon as she arrived. She came in just a little before five. I signaled to the server. He came over. I asked for the check. He went and got it and brought it back. Sometimes at night, I can still hear her crying as I walked away.

Monday morning came, I got up, got dressed, and got ready to go to work at the Texaco gas station. Things got off to a good start. There were customers who had charge accounts with the owner of the station. One of them was an undertaker. He had at least three vehicles that came in almost every week. One was a hearse, one was a limousine, and the other was a flower truck that was also used to pick up dead bodies. One day the driver of the truck came in to fill up. While the gas was going in we started talking about cremation. I told him that both my wife and I wanted to be cremated. He said, "Have you ever seen a body after it was cremated?"

I said no. he said, "I got one in there now. Would you like to see what you are going to look like?" I said yes. So he opened the box, then opened the canister, and let me take a look.

I said, "Wait a minute." I went inside the shop and came out with a substance called Stay-Dry. I looked, and they both looked the same. I said, "Gee, that makes me think." I won't need to have a burial site after I die. Just take me to the gas station, and when someone spills gas or oil on the floor, just sprinkle me on them, and we'll both disappear!

CHAPTER 14

Now ken had been offered a position from Jiffy Lube operator who had three locations in a little town called Mount Pleasant, South Carolina. He had gone down to see the locations and what his duties would be. He liked what he saw and heard, so he, Pat, and their two boys, who were grown by now, all moved to Mount Pleasant. They found a house they could rent and moved in. colleen and I were living in an apartment house on Loch Raven Road. They were there about six months. Colleen and decided to drive down over the holiday. When we got to a certain location, I had to Ken to come to meet us because he said the house was hard to reach if you didn't know the area. He met us and led us to his house. Pat had gotten a job working as a cashier for Piggly Wiggly Grocery Stores. She was very well-liked and loved her job. We stayed for a few days, and I traveled around with Ken during the day to visit the three locations. Then we traveled back to Baltimore. We stayed there till our time to serve as the head of the ladies lodge was up for Colleen and my time as chaplain was up. We decided to move to South Carolina. We told Ken. He said, "When are you planning to move?" we told him in two weeks, we just as soon as my notice was up with Len. So he rented a truck and drove up to Baltimore. Ken, Rich, and Shawn helped Colleen and me load all the furniture on the truck, and we all drove back to South Carolina. I was going to go to work at one of the Jiffy Lube shops that Ken was in charge of. Pat said she could get me hired on at Piggy Wiggley and probably Colleen too. So we arrived, put the furniture in storage, began a new life in South Carolina.

Ken found out a little later that the franchisee who owned the three Jiffy Lubes had sold them to someone else, and Ken's job was in jeopardy. Pat got me a job working in the evening and early night at the same Piggy Wiggley she worked at in the deli department. After three weeks of night work in which the only things I did was wash dishes and pans and spoons and scoops and trays and mop the floor, I had had enough Piggly Wiggley. I went the morning to a Jiffy Lube center on Johnnies Dodds Boulevard and Highway Seventeen North. The name of the new and used car sales was Miller Cadillac and Oldsmobile. As we drove by, I said, "You know what?"

She said, "What?"

I pointed over to the dealership and said, "Someday I'm going to work there."

She said, "Yeah, sure."

About two years later an ad appeared in the newspaper that read "Wanted. Experienced lubrication technician. Apply at Miller Cadillac and Oldsmobile." At lunchtime I went down and asked for an application. They gave me one, and I sat there at a desk and filled out. The shop foreman read the application said, "Why do you want to leave Jiffy Lube?"

I said, "There is no room for advancement. I've been here two years and have only gotten one raise."

He said, "How much are you making now?"

I said, "Eight dollars an hour plus commission on any additional accessories I sell."

The service manager said, "That's more money than you would make here. We would only start you at six dollars an hour."

I said, "What about additional percentage rate on any accessories sold and installed?"

He said, "Yah, you would be paid a percentage, but most people don't sell enough to amount to anything." Then he said. "I'll look over your application and give you a call in a couple of days."

Two days went by, and I not heard anything, I thought maybe the premonition I had was only wishful thinking. Two days later, the phone rang. I said, "Hello."

The voice on the other end said, "This is Miller Cadillac. Are you still interested in working here?"

I said, "Yes, sir, I shore am."

"How soon can you start?"

"I'll talk to my boss today and call you back later with an answer."

"OK," he said, "Let me know."

I talked to my boss and told him I had to let them know as soon as I could. He said, "Well, if you really want to go, you won't much good around here. Tell him the day after tomorrow."

I called, and he said, "OK, be here at eight o'clock."

I said, "Yes, sir."

I was there about fifteen minutes early. No one was there, so I banged on the door. An elderly gentleman came to the door and greeted me with a very friendly greeting. "We don't open till eight o'clock!"

I yelled back, "I'm the new lube tech, and today is my first day."

He opened the door and let me in. he said, "Sorry, but there is no one here in the shop yet. If you have a seat in the customers' lounge, someone will come and get you when they get here."

I said, "Thank you." I sat there for about twenty minutes, and finally, the man that gave me the application came in and said, "Come on I'll show you around." He took me just outside the customer's lounge. There was an area that you could park two cars in side by side with two big automatic doors, one at each end. Just before the out was an opening that led into the work area. He said, "This is where the customer comes in. There are two service writers that write up work orders. Once they are written, the vehicle is taken to the area where they will be serviced. Any questions?"

I said, "Yes, sir, where do I go to get parts and oil that I need?" He took me through an opening that led into the shop. "Here is the parts department. You tell the parts man the number of the oil filter and the amount of oil you need. He will give you the filter you need and set the gauge on the oil gun that is in your bay. And you will be ready to finish your vehicle."

So he led me all the way through the shop to the far end. There was a large door. There were cars, an SUV, and large trucks could go in and out. There was a young man there working on a car. The manager told me. "This is Ted. He will show you the ropes. Just do what he says, and follow his lead. By the way, my name is Pat."

I said, "Thanks a lot, Pat. Nice to meet you."

Ted was just finishing under the hood. He put the hood down, opened the back door, and pulled the car around on the side of the shop and put it in a parking space. He then took paperwork and keys to the parts department and came back and sat down. He looked at me and asked

"How much do you know about working on cars?" his attitude toward me made me feel like I wasn't going to be around long. He said, "You just watch me, and when I think you know what to do, I'll let you know."

I said, "Thanks. How long have you worked here?"

He said, "This is my third week. There was another guy here, but he left." I thought to myself, *With your attitude, it's no wonder he left.* The next car pulled up outside the lube bay. The driver shut the car off, got out, put a service order on the table with the keys on top of the order, and walked away. Ted just sat there. I said, "Do you want me to pull that car in and start to work on it?"

"No!" he said. "I'll tell you when you're ready to start to work on cars!" He got on the floor, set the lift arms, and raised the car up in the air. He took the wrench, opened the oil drain plug, removed the oil the filter, and went up to the parts department. He came back with the oil filter, put it on, replaced the drain plug, tightened it, and then released the lift safety switch and brought the car down. I asked, "Aren't you going to check the differential or the air pressure or even lubricate the grease fitting?"

"We don't do all of that around here, he said, "just what we have to do to get by." He put the oil filter on, put the oil in, and put the hood down. He started the car and pulled the vehicle to the finished line. I didn't want any part of a shop like that. I'll just quit and hope Jiffy Lube will take me back. I went up to the office and told Pat, "I can't work here. I am going to have to quit."

"What's wrong?" Pat asked.

"That boy back there does not lubricate any vehicles. He does not check transmission, differentials, air filters, cabin filters, or air pressure in tires, but yet he says he is doing full service?"

Pat got up out of his chair and said, "Come with me." We walked back to the service bay. Ted was sitting down as usual, reading the newspaper. Pat asked Ted, "when a car or truck comes in for a lubrication, oil change, and oil filter, just what do you do, tell me?"

Ted said, "I change the oil and the oil filter. Why?"

Pat said, "Don't you lubricate the grease fittings?"

"No," said Ted, "it's not necessary."

Pat said, "Ted, I should fire you right here and right now. But I won't. Now I'm going to put Wes in charge, and you do whatever he says." Then he turned to me and said, "You teach him how to service every vehicle that comes in here. I'm putting you in charge." Ted stayed three more days, and then he disappeared.

The next week I worked the lube rack by myself. I did a total fifteen vehicles in one day. I sold seven air filters, four cabin filters, seven tire rotations, five fuel filters, and eight sets of windshield wipers (two vehicles had rear window wiper blades, which I sold). Three of the vehicles needed brakes. (I sold the jobs but did not get to do them.) I think I proved to Pat that I knew how to do the job.

Now the man who was the overall shop foreman was named Dick. He asked me if I knew how to balance tires. I said yes, so he said that would be added to my duties. A week later Pat brought another man back to the lubrication area. He said, "Wes, this is your new helper. His name is Couze. He worked here before and left, but now he wants to come back. He will be working with you, but you will be in charge. By the way, starting today your pay increases by one dollar per hour." I thanked him for the helper and the raise.

Days, weeks, and months went by. things were going great except for one thing. When we found things wrong on the vehicles, we had to tell the service writer. The had to sell the item to the customer, the he or she got the commission on the sale. I didn't think that was fair, and I went right to Dick and told him. He said, "Fair or not, that's the way things work around here."

A year went by. Christmas was coming, and everyone was talking about the Christmas party for the employees. The party would be held on the second floor of a restaurant that was close to the shop. That was the first time I met Mr. Miller. He was at the party early, before it started, and gave Dick a bunch of envelopes to give out. He said a few words, and just before he left, Dick brought him over to the table I was sitting at. He said, "Wes, I would like to introduce you to Mr. Miller, out boss." We shook hands and said a few kind of words to each other. Then Mr. Miller asked me what I thought of the party. I said, "it's very nice except I think it would be nicer if we could have had our wives or husbands with us. But its Ok." The party lasted for four hours.

The next day work took a lot longer than it should have. Everybody was moving slower. I planned with Couze about vacations. He told me when he wanted his week off, and I told him when I wanted my week off. His time came. I worked that week alone. Things went well except for the fact that the service writers were switching tickets. They would bring back tickets that had some work for the mechanics to do and put them in front of lube and oil change vehicles. One day at lunchtime I went over to the office supply store and bought three plastic holders that would hold four of our service orders in a row on each one. I used a magic marker to write number one on the bottom to the number twelve on the top. I took stone nails and nailed them to the concrete wall. I told the service writers, put your orders in the lowest number board and hang the keys on the side with the little hook. It took almost the whole week to get them to use it. But it worked! When Couze came back from vacation, I told him how it worked.

That Saturday, we started our vacation. The kids were all excited. We had intended to drive to California in our motor home. So we packed up everything, and bright and early, we started to California. We drove all day on Sunday and had gone a pretty good distance. We stopped at the side of the Battle of Custer at the Little Big Horn. That was a very interesting visit. We started off again. We started out again on Monday and drove until I saw a sign that said "Buffalo Bill's Wild West Rodeo and Museum-five miles." I never knew five miles could take so long to drive. We got there on Monday at about 4:00 p.m. The museum closed at five, so I said, "They have a trailer park just on the other side of the road we came in on, and tomorrow we can go through the museum." Colleen and the kids all agreed. We went and checked in. The lady behind the counter said, "How long will you be staying?"

I said, "Just overnight."

She said, "That's a shame. If you were staying for two nights, you could get free tickets to go through the museum."

I looked at Colleen, she looked at me, then she looked at the lady and said, "Make it two nights. I would not want you to see my grown cowboy cry."

We got our free tickets for Wednesday. Meanwhile, we saw a sign that said "Chuck Wagon dinner Tuesday and Wednesday five to seven. Rodeo Wednesday 7:00 p.m. to 11:00 p.m. free!" So that night we had our first chuck wagon dinner-guarteer, singing Western songs and toasting marshmallows. The next day after we had eaten breakfast, we went touring the museum. There were posters and pictures from his Wild West traveling show and lots of other interesting memorabilia. Of course, the kids all needed cowboy boots and hats. We found out that night in the saloon that there was going to be reenactment of the death of Buffalo Bill the was a must see. There was a sign that read "Looking for an experience of a lifetime? Raft ride on the snake River. Details tonight at nine o'clock in the saloon!"

Well, that was all my wife (the thrill seeker) had to see. So after we had finished, we went back to the saloon. It was a very informative meeting. We learned that farting on rivers is a very interesting, thrill seeking, and dangerous sport throughout the Southwest. Rapids on the rivers are numbered from one to ten, ten being the easiest and one being the roughest and most dangerous. The Snake River was called the Big Stinky by the native Indians because it smelled like seltzer, but you will not notice it after you get into the rapids). So here was another day we were going to spend here. We went the next day by bus to the beginning of the fart riding place. Colleen, the three kids, and me were given a fifteen-minute speech on how to sit in the raft, the importance of the life jacket and helmet, and finally, what to do if you fell out of the raft. So now we were ready.

We got into the raft. Our three children were in the very front of the raft. I was seated in the second seat, and Colleen was sitting across from me. A younger woman was seated behind me, and a younger man was behind Colleen. In the very rear of the raft stood our guide. That's right! Stood not sat. We started out. The smell was so bad from the water that I thought we were all going to be sick. But it didn't last too long for we made a sharp right turn, and the bad smell of seltzer and the calm sound of the river both disappeared. The first set of rapids turned the sideways. "Pull, you people on the right," the guide yelled. Another rapid and the front of the boat was buried under the wave. And then the back end popped up. We went through six of or seven more rapids. Then the water drew strangely calm. I thought that was where we were going to stop. It was, but only for a short time. There was a large rock sticking out of the water, but water was washing around both sides and over the top. The guide said, "This is what we call sliding rock. Walk back on the beach till you see a screen with the word *start* engraved in it. Walk out into the water. You will see two metal poles sticking up out of the water. Hold on to those pools, sit down, lie back, and let go of the poles." I did, and just as soon as I let go of the poles, the current of the river carried me downstream to where the large rock was. Just before the water hit the rock, I was lifted up and slid safely over the rock and deposited on the other side with a big splash! I was safe and had a big laugh. Several other people came down after me.

It was time to get back into the raft and start on the second half of our raft ride. I thought to myself, *The second half won't be as bad as the first half.* I was right! It wasn't as bad. It was a lot worse! We hit the first rapid, and it flipped the raft sideways and into another rapid that lifted the raft into the air. When we came down, we were in a whirlpool, going round and round and round. The guide standing in the back of the raft finally got us free, and we completed our raft riding experience. We had carry our raft up and over a hill where the bus was waiting to take us back to the campground. We got back, changed into dry clothes, and then walked around trying to get our land legs back. We went to the museum, picked up some souvenirs, we went to dinner, and after we ate our second covered wagon dinner (it was better than the first), we went to the fenced-in area. There the employees put on three-hour rodeo! Bronco busting, barrel racing, bronco busting, and of course bull fighting. After the rodeo, we sat around a campfire and listened and sang best night's sleep we'd had in a long time.

Well, Colleen and I were hooked in raft riding and said we were going to go again. The next day we packed everything into the motor home and started on our way home. On the way, we passed a sign that said "Old Western town-three miles." We stopped and parked and went in to look around. I asked one of the employees there what was going on, and he said, "Well, sir, we are finishing up our snake round up. And tonight in the saloon, we are going to have boiled potatoes and fried snake."

I said, "You are actually going to eat rattlesnake meat?"

He said. "Yes, sir! When it's cooked right, it's the best."

I said to Colleen, "Honey, let's not stay."

She said, "which way is the motor home?" we drove the rest of the way home. We got there late at night, left everything in the motor home, and went to bed. Next morning we unpacked everything out of the motor home because I had made a deal with the dealer that I could park the motor home in his lot and we would not have to pay any rent if he rent it out when we were not using it. Well, the kids went their own ways, and Colleen and I were on our own. I went back to work at Miller Cadillac on Monday. First question I asked Couze was "how is the new work system working out?"

He said, "Great! I had on Oldsmobile to start working on. the work order said 'lube, oil, and filter.' I did the job, and when I was putting air in his tires, I checked the tread. Two tires had cord showing through, and the other two were completely bald. I took the paperwork up front, picked up the oil filter, and instead of going back to the lube rack, I went to the customers' lounge and asked the customer to come back to the lube rack with me because there was something I wanted to show him. I called him by his name because it was on his ticket. He came back with me, and I showed him his tires and explained to him what could happen if one of those front tires blew out at thirty-five miles per hour. He asked the price of four tires and long it would take. I said, 'if you go back up to the lounge, I'll check and let you know.' I checked. We had the tires needed. I got the price for each and added them to the price of the oil change. I went back up front to the customers' lounge, knelt down alongside him, told him the total price and that I would mount and balance them for him free, and then told him he would be on the road in one and a half hours. He said, 'Go get it done, and thanks. That's great work.'"

Things continued and got better and improved in the shop. We started to check the fuel filters while doing oil changes, but the mechanics said we were taking money out of their pockets. So we had to stop. We were changing lots of air and cabin filters. Some were easy to replace. Some were kind of hard to replace. The mechanics started doing the easy ones and left the hard ones for us to do. Things were going so well the Dick came back one day and said, "We are going to improve your working conditions. We are going to build a wash bay on the outside wall of the lube bay. Then we are going to tear down the brick wall that's between your stall and wash bay next to you so we can install another lift in there."

"Great," I said. "We'll be able to handle more vehicles that way."

Things changed, and work became more plentiful. We were doing more wiper blades because now we were checking vehicles with wiper blades on the back windows and not everybody could get them off. We were doing more tire rotations and allot more front-end alignments.

Another year went by. Another Christmas party was in the works. But this one was going to be different. Mr. Miller decided to move all the cars that were in the showroom out into the garage, clean the showroom thoroughly, and hold the party there. This year he was inviting some customers, some other VIP's (very important people), and also, this year he asked the employees to bring their wives or husbands. Now Colleen had never met Mr. Miller. So, on the night of the party, I introduced her to him. He shook hands with her and said, "Mr. Watts, one of the smartest moves I ever made was to hire your husband." The party was catered by Sticky Fingers, and the food was great.

Now things were going great. We no longer sold Oldsmobile, but we could keep on servicing them. There were lots of change in personnel. Couze had quit, and I got another man who was experienced. Then something totally unexpected happened. On Monday morning when the shop was opening for business, someone brought word that Mr. Miller had died! Later we earned that it was Mr. Miller's oldest and only son who had died. They said that he had choked to death while eating dinner with friends on Sunday. We were all sorry, but at the same, glad it was not the older Mr. Miller. After the funeral was over, we were told that Sumtter Sr. would be taking over the operation of the dealership. Things changed, but overall the transition went smooth. Now Colleen and I had been living with Pat and Ken. But like most women, she wanted a place of her own to call home. I was making more money. I had two pay raises, which brought my salary to nine dollars an hour plus commission on all additional sales. So while I was working, she went looking. One night she said to me, "I found a home I really like, but it's over in North Charleston."

I said, "What's the problem? If you like it, buy it."

She said, "I want you to see it first." So we hopped in the car and drove to North Charleston to a mobile home park. She drove one street, made a turn, and said, "There it is on the left." We went to the door, rang the doorbell, and the lady came to the door. There was a little girl at her side.

Colleen said, "Hi, I brought my husband to take at a look at your home. I hope you don't mind."

She said, "Not at all, come in." We entered and were standing in the living room. On the right side was a kitchen with a short shelf halfway up to the roof, and on the top of the shelf to the ceiling was latticework.

Halfway across the living the room on the left-hand side was a small dining area. And of course, on the right side was the kitchen. We walked back to what was the front of the mobile home, and there was a sleeping room with a small bathroom on the right side. We looked around, made a few mental changes, then walked back through the living room, which led to a small closet on the left and right alongside the closet was another bathroom. Behind that was a large back bedroom.

Collen said, "How do you like it?"

I said, "Like I told you before, it's not what oi like but what you want that counts."

She said to the lady, "Thank you. I'll call you tomorrow with our decision."

We left and talked about it on the way to Pat and Ken's house. Colleen gave the lady a check for the full amount, and she said she would be out by the end of the week. We called a mover and made arrangements to have them pick up our furniture and move it to the mobile home park. Meanwhile, Colleen had to go to Berkley County Courthouse to get a permit for the trailer and pay a month's rental fee for the month. We got everything together. Now when we were moving in, the lady who lived in the next space was working out in her yard in a pair of shorts and a tank top. She said, "Hi, are you my new neighbors?"

I said, "Yes, we are."

She said, "Good to have you." And we continued carrying in our food and clothes and groceries. The lady next door continued to work in her garden. When we finally got everything in the house, Colleen turned to me and asked, "Did you see our next-door neighbor working in her garden?"

I said, "Yes."

"Did she talk to you?"

I said, "Yes. She said hi and welcome."

She said, "Well, she didn't say anything to me! So don't talk to her." I thought she was kidding and didn't think any more about it.

Monday rolled around, and I got to work. One of the other employees said, "Hey, Wes, how do you like your new home?"

I said, "It's great, but it sure in one long drive."

He said. "How come?"

I replied, "Well, I live in North Charleston, but I work in Greece!"

He said, "Oh very funny."

During the week, going and coming was a quiet time just to drive and meditate. As soon as I pulled up in front of the house, Colleen would be at the door to make sure I was not talking to the woman next door. Friday rolled around, and I got home, ate dinner, watched TV, then went to bed. I got up on Saturday, ate breakfast, and said, "Are you ready to go to the grocery store?"

she said, "Not quite." So finally, she said, "OK, I'm ready" We walked out the door. I turned to lock the door, and when I turned to go down the steps, the lady next door, who was working in her garden, looked up and said, "Hi neighbor, is everything going OK?"

I said, "Yes, thanks," and got in the car. Out of nowhere I heard, "What did you have to talk to her for? Why can't you just ignore her?"

I said, "Don't be ridiculous! All I did was answer a question."

Things kept getting worse. Sometimes I just felt like staying and working for nothing just so I wouldn't have to go home.

A few days later Colleen said she had a terrible pain in her head. I called in sick and took her to the doctor's office. He saw her, gave her an examination, then told her to go into the other room with the nurse. He came back into the room with me and gave me the news that she had Alzheimer's disease. He said he wanted to set her up with a hospice program where people would come out three times a week and examine her and report back to him. I agreed and signed the papers. He gave her prescription for something for her nerves to calm her down. We went home, and I got the medicine for her.

Things went OK for the next couple of days, then one day, I got a phone call from my oldest son, Ken. He said that his son Richard, who was a police officer for the North Charleston Police Department, had driven over to the house to check on Colleen. He found her lying at the foot of the steps, and she couldn't get up. He immediately called EMS, and they sent an ambulance and took her to the hospital. Then he called ken, and Ken called me. I told my boss what happened. I had to go. He said, "Go!"

When I got to the hospital, Ken was already there. colleen was sitting up in the bed, talking to anyone and everyone and not making any sense at all. I asked Ken what was happening, and he said the doctor had given her a shot to calm her down. But it had done just the opposite. It made her loopy. We stayed there an hour, and finally, the doctor released her. After that we took her home, and Ken said something about selling the mobile home and moving back with them. Doing something quite unlike her, Colleen agreed.

Colleen had heard about a place near Pennsylvania called the Ohiopyle River. She wanted to go raft riding. I put in for my vacation from work. It was granted. I told Tammy, our daughter, what Colleen wanted. She agreed to go, and her husband, Dan, said he would go too. So we left Friday, drove up to Pennsylvania, found the place, and signed up to go raft riding on Sunday. They had a place to stay overnight in our motor home, so we stayed. Sunday morning, we went to get instructions on rafting in this river. Now this river, the Ohiopyle, is rated a three on the scale of one (the worst) to ten (the easiest). So we were given the instructions. Don't stand up. Keep your feet locked in under the side of the raft. And don't stand up. So we put on our safety vest and helmet took off our shoes. Colleen and I were in the front of the raft with Dan and Tammy in the back of the raft. We started out. We went through one rapid and made out OK. We broke through another OK and came through two or three more. We started into a big one, and before anyone could realize, Colleen was gone. She had fallen out of the raft and could not be found. Now she could swim, but there was no way in these rapids. She could not hold her breath for very long. We got to one side near a big rock where the water was calm. Tammy was calling and crying. Dan was yelling at the top of his voice. I was looking, bellowing, and crying all at the same time. At least ten minutes had gone by, and I thought, *She is gone.* Then I prayed, "Oh, Jesus, why? Why did you have to take her like this? Please, God, if there is any way to bring her back, I will do whatever it is you want me to do. But please, God, send her back." I looked down into the water and saw her face coming up out of the water! My heart skipped two beats as I reached for her. He had heard my prayer! He truly does care! Thank you, thank you, God! These were the words that were in my heart. He really does answer prayer.

We spent that night in the camper, and when Tammy and Dan were asleep, I asked Colleen, "How did you do it? How could you possibly hold your breath that long?"

She said, "I could hear you calling, but I could not answer. I could feel you all walking all over me when I was trying to find my way up. But I just could not get loose. Then I just popped up." Well, the "thank you, Jesus" and the "I'll serve you" just went clear out of my head.

We got up the next morning and headed to Baltimore. Our rafting days were over. We moved back in with Pat and Ken, sold the motor home, sold the camper, and just went about every day like it was normal. Now Collen's mother and her sister Pat were both in nursing homes when they died. She begged me to never put her in a nursing home. I promised I would not. Some promises can't be kept.

CHAPTER 15

Now more time had gone by, and Colleen was getting worse. Some days would be good, others would be bad, and some would be just horrible. One night I woke up out of a sound sleep. Colleen was gone. I looked in the bathroom, in the kitchen, in the living room, and even in the backyard. No Colleen. I went to the front door. It was unlocked. The outside light was on. I went outside, and there she was trying to catch her little dog Dusty. She had raised that dog from a puppy. He was friendly, very playful, and good with kids of all ages. But to anyone touching or yelling at Colleen, he would somehow always get between her and whoever it was as if he was going to protect her. Ken and Pat came out. I thought we were going to wake the whole neighborhood. We finally got them in.

Now a couple of days went by, and the nurse came to visit her. I don't know to this day what she said or what she saw, but she reported that Colleen should be under daily supervision. The head lady met with me on Friday during lunchtime. She said she had a place for Colleen in downtown Charleston. She gave me some paperwork and told me to take her there on Monday. So on Monday I told her I was taking her downtown for an examination. When we got there, she saw the name on the building, and she said, "I'm not going in there! You think I am crazy! You're not going to put me in there!"

I told her, "This is where they do the testing. You're not going to be here long." I did not lie about that part because the lady from hospice said the place could only hold her for one week. So I took her in, saw the head nurse, and gave her the paperwork. She took the paperwork and asked me to sit next to Colleen while they got a room ready for her. After about a half hour went by, the nurse came over and said, "Mrs. Watts, come with me please. Mr. Watts, you may go."

Well, I walked with her until we came to a hallway that had a sign the read "Exit." I followed the sign. The nurse took her the other way, and by the time I was about to leave, she came running up the aisle. The head nurse and a large man came up with her. The man held her by the arms. The head nurse said, "You do know, sir, that the doctors do not want her to have visitors during the week while they are working with her. But you can come own on Saturday to pick her up."

I said OK, and they both escorted her to a room down the hall, put her in it, and locked the door. I could still hear her screaming when I reached the far end of the flower garden.

When I got home, there was her little dog Dusty, waiting at the door. After I went in, he wanted to see if she was coming in. it was a very difficult week at work. That week the hours just dragged. I could not get anything right. Finally, Friday came around. I went to meet the hospice nurse, and she said, "You're lucky, Mr. Watts. I was able to get the hospital to hold Colleen for another week."

I said, "I guess that's OK but I was supposed to pick her up on Saturday. Now you're telling me I can't?"

She said, "It's for her own good, and the extra week will help her a lot."

I agreed, but I did not like it. So Saturday when I went in, she was nowhere to be found. The head nurse called security. They looked, but there was no trace of her. After an hour of searching, she came out of her room. I saw her, ran to her, and hugged and kissed her. I said, "Where were you? Everybody has been looking for you!"

She said, "I was hiding under my bed. I wanted to scare them."

We sat and talked and held hands for two hours. Then the nurse came and told me my time was up. I kissed Colleen and said goodbye. She kissed me back and said goodbye. I walked up to the door to go, and somebody hollered, "Don't open that door!" I turned to see who was hollering, and Colleen was right behind me. They came and got her and put her in her room and locked the door. I left wiping my eyes as I walked.

Another Monday came around. Another week of wonder and worry. Finally, it was Friday and another visit with the hospice nurse. She explained to me that the doctors at that hospital could not get her to cooperate with them and that they had little or no success with her. So she said, "There is another hospital that handles nothing but hospice patients, but it's up in northwest part of North Charleston." When she gave me the address, I said I knew just where it was. Sha gave me some paperwork and told me to take Colleen there on Sunday and that they would take care of her, but again, no visit during the week. So I took her up there straight from the first hospital. We got there. I took her inside, dropped her off, and visited with her as long as I could. Then a nurse came and got her and said I should leave while she was being evaluated. I kissed her goodbye and left.

It was another long, long week. It seemed the days were getting longer and that time was moving slower. All this time I was missing church on Sundays. It did not occur to me that I was breaking the first commandment ("I am the lord thy God. You shall have no other gods before me!") and also the second commandment ("Remember the Sabbath and keep it holy"). So Monday came, and work was piling up. I stayed late a couple of nights trying to catch up. But nothing seemed to help. Friday rolled around, and again, at lunchtime I met with the hospice nurse. She said that she had a friend who owned a home for people with hospice and others. She said it was expensive, but if I wanted her to, she would talk to her friend and see if they could take Colleen. I said I would appreciate any help at all.

So on Saturday I drove out to see Colleen, and she was sitting up on the side of her bed, waiting. I said hi and kissed her. She said "Hi! I missed you!" we sat and talked about the past week. Finally, she said, OK, I'm ready. Let's go!"

"Go where?" I asked.

She replied, "Go home. I'm all well now."

We walked around a little while and sat outside in the garden for a little while. Then she headed for the front door. A nurse stopped her, and she started screaming and hollering. They took her back to her bed, strapped her in so she could not get up, and gave her a shot to calm her down. The nurse said, "Mr. Watts, that shot is going to calm her down, and she will be sleeping for about two hours. But the head nurse wants to see you in her office." So I went there. She said that the hospice had made arrangements for Colleen to be kept there for another week. But I would have to pay three hundred dollars. I had my cash from my paycheck (was that just luck? Or was God getting me prepared?). I gave her the money, then left.

On the way home I got to thinking, *It's been a long while since I have been to church on Sunday morning. I think I'll go tomorrow before I come out here*. I did. I don't remember anything the preacher said or anything the choir sang, but I do remember the peace I left. After church I drove out to the hospital and had a few good hours with my wife. Dinnertime came, and they came and took her to eat. I figured that was a good time to leave, so I did. On Monday I received a phone call from the hospice nurse. The lady at the home had an opening and wanted to meet with me to make arrangements. She asked if I could meet with her on Tuesday at noon and that we could go together and see if I thought Colleen would be happy there. So we did. I met the owner and she was also the head nurse. We talked about the kind of help she would be getting and about the cost. She told me that what she Medicare paid was two hundred dollars a month under what she charged. So I would have to pay the amount by cash or check on the first of each month. I said that would be OK. I could handle it. We filled out the paperwork and all the releases and prescription information. We shook hands, and I asked if I could bring Colleen in on Saturday. She said yes.

So Saturday rolled around like it does every week. But this time, driving out wasn't too bad. I knew I would have her in the car with me coming back. I picked her up, and we drove back slowly so we could spend some time together. I even stopped and bought her a large chocolate milkshake. We got to the home. We went in, and I introduced them to each other. We sat down, and they talked. I just Sat there and held her hand. After a while the head lady took us to the room that was going to her new home. We went back to the office. She gave me more papers to sign, then she said she had to show me something else. She took me to the front door and said it would be best if I left now. I said, "Will it be OK to come tomorrow?" she said yes. I asked about visiting hours during the week, and she said visiting hours were any time between 9:00 a.m. and 6:00 p.m. because they had church on Sunday morning and did not want people coming in while church was being held. So I left.

While driving home I was thinking, *Well, that's good for me because now I can go to church on Sunday morning, come visit Colleen, and be able to get back to church on Sunday night.* So I left and went home. Sunday morning I got up, got dressed, and headed to Awendaw, to the First Baptist Church of Awendaw. Of course, everyone, including the pastor, wanted to know if everything was OK, how Colleen was doing, and how I was holding up. Well, the pastor gave me some time to go to the pulpit and let whole church know at the same time. The pastor brought the sermon to us. And when church was over, I had to drive an extra twelve miles from Awendaw back to Mount Pleasant to start my fifteen-mile trip to North Charleston and the nursing home.

So Colleen's birthday came around, and I ordered a birthday cake big enough to serve fifty people and stopped to pick up fifty small cups of vanilla ice cream. And when I got over there that Saturday, we had a big birthday party for her. She was really surprised and angry.

I said to her, "What are you angry about? And why are you mad at me?"

She looked at me and said, "For sixty years of our marriage, I took the children to the beach for a week so no one would remember my birthday, and here you blow it by bringing a cake and ice cream just to let everyone know it's my birthday."

Monday came, and before I started, I went to Dick's office and asked to speak to him. He said, "Come on in and close the door." I went in, closed the door, and sat down. I told him about the visiting hours and how I would not be going to see Colleen doing the week. He said, "We'll work something out. Mr. Miller and I were talking about the job you have done since you've been here, and he suggested giving you a raise. How does that sound?"

I said, "Just great!"

He said, "Good. Starting today your hourly wage goes to twelve dollars and fifty cents an hour. Plus 10 percent commission on all accessories and labor you sell." I thanked him, we shook hands, and I left.

The following Thursday he called me into his office and said, "I need you to do a favor for me. We have a blue Cadillac that they need up at the north store. Can you drive that car up there and drop it off? They will give you another vehicle to bring back here. I'm not sure how long it will take, but I think you can do it in about two hours."

I looked at him puzzled, and said, "What's the matter?"

I said, "And I never thought you liked me."

"Get out of here," he said. so I drove to the north store, left the blue car, got a jeep, and started back. That had taken a half hour. So I drove around the corner, down two blocks, and what do you know? There was a nursing home, and I had a whole hour to visit.

Time went by, and later Mr. Miller Sr. passed away. His son-in-law, summer Sr., took over the operation.

Another two years went by, and on one Friday, I took a small cake and two small ice-cream cups to the nursing home and went in. the hospice nurse was there, and I said to her, "We are celebrating our wedding anniversary."

She looked at Colleen and said, "That's real nice, Colleen. How long have you been married?"

Colleen looked at her and replied, "Forever."

Another month went by, and we celebrated New Year's Eve together. On January 29, I got the phone call I had dreaded for over two years. "Wes, Colleen I gone," the voice said. it was after two o'clock in the morning.

"Where did she go?" I asked

The voice said, "she passed away."

I said, "I'll be right over."

Someone once told me that just before you pass away, your whole life passes before your eyes. Well, I don't know if that is true or not, but I do know that by time I got dressed and got to the car, the last sixty-two years of my life did. I asked the question, "Why, God? Why did you take her now?" let me tell you something you don't really want to know! He took control of the car. I was crying so hard I couldn't see. He answered, "Do you remember the raft ride on the Ohiopyle River? The time Colleen fell out of the raft for no reason? That was her time to die! You said yourself she could not hold her breath that long. She was destined for heaven. But you, Tammy, and Dan prayed so hard and with so much love and compassion that I changed my mind and added another seventeen years to her life. Now do you understand?" He knew I did because I knew and was thankful for the extra time.

I came back into myself just as I turned the car into the parking lot. I got out, went to the door, and the young man that was on duty opened the door and escorted me to her room. As I walked into the room, I looked at her lying there so still and quiet. I looked at her face, and there was a small opening along the bottom of her eyes. The two men in the room, the coroner and the undertaker, left the room. I sat down on the bed, took her body in my arms, and kissed her lips. That would not be the last time I kissed her lips, but it was the last time her heart would be in it. When the men came back into the room, laid her body down and saw that her eyes were closed and she was smiling. I left and, all the way home, thanked God for every one of our sixty-two years together.

I called in to work the next day and told them what happened and that I was going to need a few days off to make final arrangements. Pat and Ken very helpful over the next few days. We selected the clothes she was to be cremated in and took them to the crematorium. We selected some jewelry that the girls could put ashes in, and we are as a memorial. We picked out flowers for the altar and an urn for the ashes. We decided to get a caterer to handle the food and drink part. And we contacted our pastor to handle the funeral process. Pat sang a couple of hymns. Ken had some parts to tell. I tried to tell all I could without crying. The service was over. But not quite! You see, she served two years as head lady of the Moose Lodge, and she had made it very clear to me that she wanted her ritual. So what did she want? Call the Moose Lodge in Maryland and plan a memorial service with food and drink. Contact the pastor of Joppa Road Baptist Church and have him conduct the ritual, not the present pastor but the one that was there when we joined the church. Then we were to take her ashes and sprinkle them over her mother's and father's grave. Seven days after her funeral, we had completed her requests.

I had gone back and taken my vacation time to deal with the funeral. Now it was time to leave the past and get on with the future. Now I started going back to Awendaw Church. The pastor had retired and had his assistant replace him. Attendance kept dropping. He left, and the church voted to ordained pastor that worked full-time for the Baptist association to be a Sunday morning and Sunday night and Wednesday night minister. That worked for a while but no long. We used to hold choir practice on Wednesday night at six thirty. When Wednesday night services were stopped so was choir practice. We started holding practice after Sunday evening services.

One Sunday morning the choir director asked me to join the choir. I refused, but she was very insistent. So finally, I said OK. So she said, "Look it's no sense for the three of us to drive three cars up to Awendaw. Let's set a location. We'll meet there and just take one car." We all agreed. Then she said, "Wes, you live near the Palms, don't you?"

I said, "Yes."

She said, "How about you picking up Eulalie and I'll meet you at Harris Tetter parking lot and we will all go up together?" Now Eulalie was a very nice lady. Part of my job as a church deacon was to visit church members and families in a certain area. Now Ann, the choir director, and Eulalie and her husband, George, lived in the area that my wife and I were assigned to visit. Now Eulalie's husband had passed away two years earlier from asbestos poison. So she lived in an apartment at the Palms. So on Sunday evenings I would drive to the Palms, pick up Eulalie, and drive to Harris Tetter parking lot. This went on for about two months. One Sunday morning I walked into the Sunday school room with a small black bucket in my hand, and I sat it on the long table that everyone sat around. Everyone looked, and finally someone asked what the bucket was for. I pulled the sheet music book out of the bucket and said, "When I was in school, the music teacher told me I could not carry any tune in a bucket. This just proves she was wrong about me." Everyone burst out laughing.

Now time went by, and all of a sudden, Ann, the choir director, had to go up to church earlier than Eulalie and me. So she said she would meet us up there. So we rode the twelve miles up the road. We didn't speak one word going up and only said good night after we got back. Eulalie and I continued to ride back and forth together and started to talk more.

Meanwhile, we got word at work that the dealership was being put up for sale. Then we heard a bid had been placed from another dealer. Finally, things were settled. It was true. Miller Cadillac had been sold, and a new dealer would be taking over by the first of the month. We were also told not to worry that even though he was taking control on the first of the month, there would not be any changes made for at least a month. So things continues as they were for a while.

Meanwhile, Eulalie stopped ridding with me to choir practice, and I thought maybe I had said something to offend her. Then the preacher said she was in the hospital. I went to see her and found out from the front desk what room she was in. I pushed the button for the elevator, and made some comments about how they liked the shirt I had on. They got off the elevator on the same floor and walked down the hall to the same room as me. We all had a big laugh. They were her niece and grandmother. She was moved to Savana Grace Rehab. I would go home after work, eat dinner, clean up and change my clothes, and then drive to where she was, and we would play five hundred rummy. This went on for about three weeks, and then she was released. She went back to the Palms to her old apartment. I would come to visit her in the evenings, and we would play cards and talk. One Sunday night I brought her home from choir practice and when we got to door, I stopped the car, walked around to her side of the car, opened her door, and helped her out. When she straightened up, I put my arms around her and kissed her. Then I said, "I'm sorry." She said, "I'm not." So I kissed her again. Then she invited me up to her apartment, and we talked about life alone. I left that night a little after 11:00 p.m. When I got to the front door, it was locked. I remembered that there was a garden in the middle of the apartment building and figured that was a good place to get out. I walked all around that garden, and there walls of apartments on all sides. I went back to the front desk thinking that the caretaker would be there, but he wasn't. I knew there was an office in the back room behind the desk and thought maybe the caretaker was back there. I went around front desk and opened the door. There was the office but no caretakes. I saw a door and said to myself silently, "Lord, please let that door lead outside." He did, and it did.

I got into my car and drove around to Hidden Bridge Drive. It was after midnight when I got into the house. Pat and Ken were still up, and Pat said, "Hi, Dad, you're a little late tonight, aren't you?"

I said, "I didn't know I had a curfew to keep." I said good night and went to bed.

I got up the next day, went to work, and noticed a lot of new people walking around checking the equipment. I asked one of the mechanics what was going oi. He said they were making an appraisement on the equipment. They finished and left, and the day went on. Quitting time came. I cleaned my area and left. I stayed home that night. Talked to Eulalie on the telephone, and asked her if she would like to go on a picnic on Saturday about noon. She said that sounded good. So Saturday came, and I drove to the Palms, called her on the phone, and said, "I'm downstairs."

She said, "I'll be right down." And she was. So we drove to the bridge, but instead of going over the bridge, we went under the bridge. Now for some reason, the wind was blowing, and it was cold. We started to walk holding hands, but the wind didn't want any part of that. So we stopped in the coffee shop and had cups of hot chocolate. So that was our first date. We went back to the Palms, and she said, "Do you want to come up for a while?"

I said, "Sure."

When we got in, I sat in a rocking recliner, and she came over and sat on my lap. I was holding her and out of a clear blue sky asked her, "Have you ever thought about getting married, and if you did, would you think about marrying me?"

She said yes. I asked, "Yes to what? Getting married or marrying me?"

She said, "Yes to both." We kissed and just sat and thought about how we were going to tell each other's family and how we were going to tell the church. Well, I went home and told Pat and Ken, and of course, they said, "It's a little soon, don't you think?"

I said, "When you find someone to love and that same loved one loves you back at our ages, you don't wait, you act." And besides we really didn't need permission.

So Sunday came, and I was supposed to make the announcements from the pulpit. Now Eulalie was supposed to be there. But something happened, and she could not be there. So on Sunday morning, all through Bible study and through the first hymn, I kept thinking, *How can I say this?* Finally, it was time for announcements. I got behind the pulpit so the people couldn't see my knees shaking. I made all the announcements and started to walk away, then stopped, turned back, and said, "Sorry, folks, I almost forgot one thing. Mrs. Eulalie is going to get married, and she wanted to me be sure to invite all of you to the wedding. It will be here at the church on July 16 at 1:00 p.m. You are all invited to attend. The reception will be held at the fellowship hall immediately after the service."

Well, before I could even finish, the congregation was buzzing. I started to walk away, stopped, turned toward them, and said, "By the way, the man she is going to marry is me." They all screamed. So we told Eulalie's family and they were all happy. Surprised but happy. Her daughter Cathy took care of decorating the fellowship hall and getting the arranged, the wedding cake too. All Eulalie and I had to do was show up.

Now our former pastor, who knows me quite well, asked her three times, "Are you sure you want to go through with this?" she said yes every time.

Now Miller Cadillac was sold another dealer. And he held a meeting with all the employees and said, "Nothing is going to change right away. In six months we will be building a new location on the other side of the bridge. You are all welcome to stay and move over when the time comes." Everybody agreed to stay the six months, then make a final decision.

Meanwhile, Eulalie and I went on our honeymoon. She had a good friend who lived in Tennessee and was in the hospital. We drove over there and stayed in a motel for three days while we visited with her friend. Then we left, and on the way back, we stopped for a day at the Christ Museum in Gathlandberg, Tennessee. We spent a day and a half there. When we came back to the Palms, people were asking us how long we had been married. I kiddingly told them, "One hundred and twenty years. And if you ask how long to each other, it's one month."

When Colleen was still alive, she always asked me, "If I die before you, would you get married again?" I had not really thought about it, but I told her probably not.

She said, "I'll bet you won't be single for six months."

Eulalie and I got married five months and three weeks after her death. I didn't know she was a prophet. Now since Eulalie and I have been married, God has been using us to serve him. When we got married, she was living at the Palms of Mount Pleasant in room number 215. After a while I said, "This doesn't make any sense at all. You have a house of Riffle Range Road that your nephe§w lives in for free, and we pay all this money for rent. Give him notice that we are going to move in."

She told him and told him when we wanted to move in. she had put the house up for sale, but the real estate agents were not showing the house. So we called the moving company and made arrangements to move on a certain date at a certain time. The moving men came and loaded the truck, and we gave them the address. We, meanwhile, turned in our keys to the apartment. We drove to the house. Her nephew was moving the last stuff out. The moving truck pulled up, the TV installer pulled up, and the real estate lady showed up. And we were there.

The real estate lady said to Eulalie, "I have someone interested in your house. He will be here soon."

I said, "She's not going to sell. We're just moving in." (Now you may think that God does not work in mysterious ways, but this house had been on the market, and no one even looked at it.) Now two pickup trucks pulled up. It was the person who wanted to buy the house and his real estate agent. He wanted to look around. I told him he was welcome to look, but she probably would not sell. So he said he really wanted to look at the old market that was on the property. Eulalie and I had been going over to the house and cleaning out a lot of stuff that her first husband, George, and his brother, Peewee, used to use. I unlocked the door. He and his agent looked around and asked where the property ended. Then he said, "I'll take it. It's just what I've been looking for."

He said, "What about that trailer over there? Is that on your property?"

I said, "Yes, it is, but we have an order to vacate in thirty days."

Meanwhile the TV man finished. The moving men were done and waiting for their check. The real estate lady was talking to Eulalie. And I was talking to the prospective buyer. Things were moving fast. The prospective buyer and his agent talked to the real estate agent. She came over to Eulalie and said, "He really wants this property. He said it was exactly what he wanted and he is willing to pay full price."

Eulalie looked at me and asked what I thought. I said, "You said you wanted the full price for the house and the land. You said you did not want to stay here, so this is a chance to get rid of the responsibility and sell." She signed the papers. We still moved in.

We did not know it at the time, but God was pulling all the strings. First, we moved in. then gave the young man living in the trailer thirty days notice to evict the property. He never sent to his mailbox to pick up his mail. The box was running over. I asked the mail carrier to please post it on his back door because he never used the front door. He did, and I thanked him. The thirty days went by, nothing happened. We went to the magistrate's office. The lady there said, "We have to notify the sheriff's office, and they have to make sure he got the notice." So when we talked to the sheriff's deputy, he said they had to give him thirty days notice. Meanwhile, the inspector from the bank came and inspected the house and the property and sent a fax to the realtor that we had to have a termite inspection, a survey of the property, and the removal of the trailer off the property. The real estate people said they would take care of everything.

My Life in God's Hands

Now we had moved in to the house in May. It was now in July, and the trailer had not been touched. The sheriff's deputy finally got hold of the boy that lived in the camper and said, "You have to vacate the property by 5:00 p.m. this evening. After that Mr. Watts takes claim of the trailer and anything left in it and anything left on the property." The deputy told Eulalie and me that he could do nothing after that evening, but he would be there at nine o'clock the next morning. He was also with two police officers and a locksmith. The locksmith started to change the lock and said, "This lock doesn't even work."

The sheriff said, "Let me try," he pushed on the door, and nothing happened.

He said, "It must be barred from the inside." One of the police officers who was a little on the broad side said, "Let me try to get it opened." He took two good hits with his shoulder on the door, and it flew open.

He looked inside and said, "I'm not going in there." I looked inside, and right inside the door a whole section of the floor was gone. A big hole through to the ground. The sheriff's deputy and I stepped around the hole. We walked through the trailer room by room. It was a total disgrace. Everything inside that could be removed was removed. There were holes in three rooms on the floor, and the one room that still had a complete floor had a mattress on it. Junk was everywhere. I asked the deputy what I should do with it. He said, "Whatever is here you put out on the side of the road. Stack it neat, then whatever happens is not your responsibility." I took the wheel barrel that left there and put it out by the front door.

The I threw everything out the door and into the wheel barrel. When it was full, I took it over to the side of the road and dumped it. Eulalie and I had a doctor's appointment that afternoon. So I had to stop, clean up, and change my clothes, and then off to the doctor's we went. When we got back, I went down to the trailer, and all the junk was gone. I said, "Thank you, Lord, I do not have to fool with that."

A week later we a got call from the buyer's agent. The move had taken longer than it should, and the buyer wanted to move in so he didn't have to move twice. We called the Palms and talked to the saleslady. She said they had one apartment empty on the first floor. It was apartment 111. We said, "We'll take it." We called the moving company that had moved us out, and when I told the lady the name Watts, she said, "Didn't we just move you a few month's ago?" well, it's to be known. The move was scheduled for the next day. I called the client's agent and said he could move in that afternoon. So the next day we were back at the Palms in room 111. Now when we moved back, we took the first-floor apartment. When we went to bed at night at about 10:30 p.m., we noticed a light shining in our kitchen ceiling. I got up to turn it off. There was no light in the apartment on. We thought it was a car coming in to park. Again the next night, the light appeared again and stayed on for one minute. Again the next night, the light came on at ten thirty and stayed on for two minutes. I saw Jack the maintenance manager and asked him if it could be a light showing in from outside. He thought it could be the light on the microwave oven flashing, so he replaced it. The light came back at ten thirty. We had Jack come back again to check. He could not find any way there could be light coming into the apartment.

Eulalie was all nervous about the light, so we talked to Ashley, one of the salespeople. She said there was a two-bedroom, two bath apartment on the third floor and it was empty and ready. So the next day I called the mover and told them we wanted to move from the first floor to the third floor. They provided the same two that moved us in. And when we went to bed and ten thirty came around, guess what? Yep, that's right. The light showed on the kitchen ceiling at ten thirty and again at eleven thirty and again at twelve thirty. Eulalie wants to know where the light comes from. I am willing to accept the Bible description that "those who walk in the light must live in the light." And I am thankful that we get to see the light.

There are a couple of other things that have happened in our lives I would like to tell you about. The first one is about Colleen, my first wife. When she passed away in 2012, I read the death certificate, and it said that she was born at 1133 Homestead Street. I lived at 1130 Homestead Street. Remember the little Colleen from the tea parties? Just a coincidence or God's plan? Remember, my mother said, "The only way you will marry that girl is over my dead body!" she died three months later! Did it just happen that way? Or was it God's will? Remember the word I heard at the gas station when I was pretending to put gas in my tricycle-*Wait?* The two men in 1966 offering me my own service station? (did it just happen that way, or was it God's will?) so many unanswered questions! How can you explain them? And after Eulalie and I got married and I moved into the Palms, on Sunday afternoon at four thirty in the afternoon, we have a service called vespers. It simply means "evening religious services." There was a doctor living at the Palms. His name was Dr. Wells. He was a very deep religious preacher. He would do one service a month, usually on the first Sunday. There were three other clergy preachers who came on the other three Sundays. One was a lady. Eulalie and I started attending those services. And we still do. But for some reason unknown to me, Dr. Wells held my attention. Now there is still a resident who lives here that always leads the hymn singing for Dr. Wells. One Sunday, as we all gathered in the auditorium waiting for Dr. Wells to come, Phill made an announcement that Dr. Wells was sick and would not be coming. He immediately walked back six rows to the end seat where I was sitting and asked me to fill for Dr. Wells.

Now when I was in school, I hated to have to get up and speak to the class. Things hadn't changed. I still did not want to get up and try to lead a worship service. I did not look up, but I got up. I walked the longest aisle I had ever walked, and before I could open my mouth, my brain said, "What are you going to talk about?" My mind was blank. I said a very little and quick prayer. "Lord, I can't do this. Please help me!" Something happened. Out of my mouth came the words "let's begin with a word of prayer!" After that I started with the words "serving God is like being on a baseball team. You sit in the dugout, waiting for your change to pinch-hit. And one day the manager (God) points his finger at you and says, 'Get a bat, get in the box, and get a hit!' You pick up your bat (your Bible), and as you waltz to the batter's box, the third-base coach (Jesus) comes over to you and whispers, 'Get in there, and get your hit (translation in religious beliefs-"I can do all things through Christ who strengthens me"). So you step up to the plate. The pitcher (Satan) throws an outside curve ball that just catches the plate. "Strike one," the umpire calls. Then you feel it. That little voice inside you repeats those words you heard before-'I can do all things through Christ who strengthens me.' Here it comes, right over the heart of the plate. You swing. Contact! Your swing was late, but you hit the ball! You run to first. The coach is yelling, 'keep going.' You step on first and start for second and head for the third. The fielder throws the ball to the second-base man. He drops the ball. You head around third and are o our way home! Will you make it? Can you succeed? Sorry, everyone, the game isn't over yet. I can't say if it was a home run or a force out at the plate. Only the father can tell you. Will you ever play in the game? Who knows? But the real question is, when he calls, will you be willing? Let us pray."

That was my first vesper service. Since then all the leaders who used to be here have left. But God does provide. We now have five individuals who each get one Sunday a month to lead. Now you probably think I made a mistake. It should be four, not five. No, there four months that have five weeks in a year. And besides it never hurts to have someone ready in the dugout.

There is another answer God has given to Eulalie and me. Back some time ago, the church we went to lost their piano player. For a while we tried to sing without music, but that just didn't do the trick. So our choir director made up a book of hymns that she wanted to get music made to. We tried but everyone who could play an organ or a piano was booked up for Sunday. So Eulalie and were going to the church on Tuesday to do some gardening. We put an ad in the paper for a piano player to call if "you can play the piano for two hours on Tuesday, we will pay twenty dollars." We received seven (the number of completion) calls. We selected the first caller. We said for her to meet us at first Baptist Church of Awendaw and gave her directions. She came and said her name was Janice, and we showed her the list of hymns we wanted her to record. She said OK. Sometime later, Eulalie and went outside to work on the front garden. About an hour later, we went in to get some water, and we stopped by to see how she was doing. She was sitting at the piano playing music that I did remember on the list I gave her. She said, "All done, "and handed me the disks. I asked if she would like to come and play in person for our church on Sunday morning.

She said, "No, sir, I play at my own church on Sunday morning."

So I handed her an envelope with the agreed price in it. She said, "Thank you."

I said, "You're very welcome. They sound great. If we need you to play again, may I call you?"

She said, "Sure."

Later on that week I called her phone number again. She answered and said, "Hello."

I said, "Hi, Janice, this is Wes from Amendaw Church. I know you said you play for your church on Sunday morning. But would you be able to play for us on Sunday from four thirty till five o'clock?"

She said, "At your church?"

I said, "No, this is at Palms where we live."

She said, "Yes, sir, I can do that."

I said, "Great! See you Sunday at four thirty."

She came, she played, and everyone fell in love with her and with her playing. When service was over, I went to thank her and handed her envelope with the payment we agreed on, and she said, "What's this?"

I said, "It's what we agreed on."

She said, "I don't want this."

I said, "It's what we agreed on. Please take it along with our thanks."

She has continued to come not only for Eulalie and me but for other ones that do vespers and also for the service we do over at assistant living on the second Wednesday of every week of the month.

Well, this is one more story. Eulalie and I moved again from the first floor to the third floor. She was getting upset about that light that was showing up every night. We moved into a two-bedroom, two-bath apartment. The second bedroom is more of a storage room. The first night we were in our new apartment, number 359, we had a guest. Yes, it was and still is the bright light that shines at night just below our air-conditioning duct, two to three times a night starting at about ten thirty until we fall asleep. What causes the light? No one knows. But it's there. God put it there. And I will wonder, but I won't worry. Why? Because Jesus said, "I am the light of the world. No one sees the light unless my Father calls them."

Thank you for buying this book. Be true to God, and he will be true to you.

Our Wedding Day

**

Our Fiftieth Anniversary

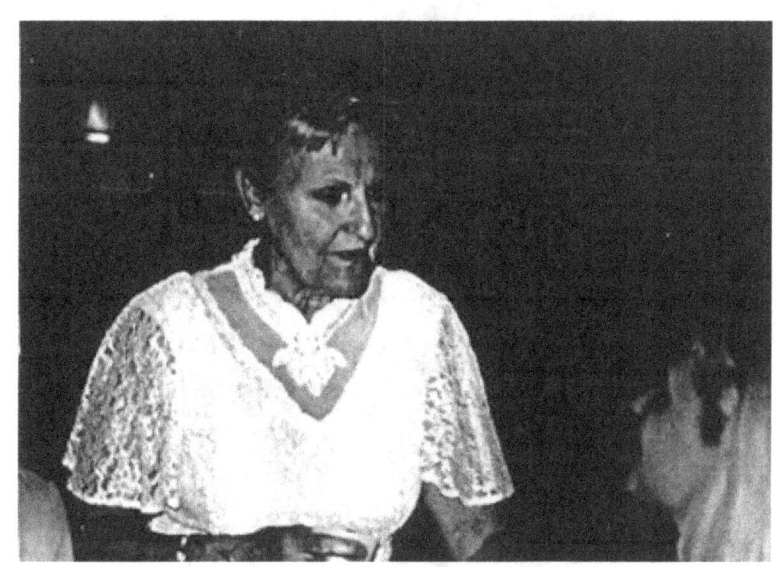

Colleen

Daughter Cindy

Son Ken, and his wife, Pat
Fiftieth Wedding Anniversary

Dan, son-in-law
Tammy, daughter

On vacation

Cowboy Wes and His Lady Colleen

Colleen and me on
our fiftieth wedding invitations

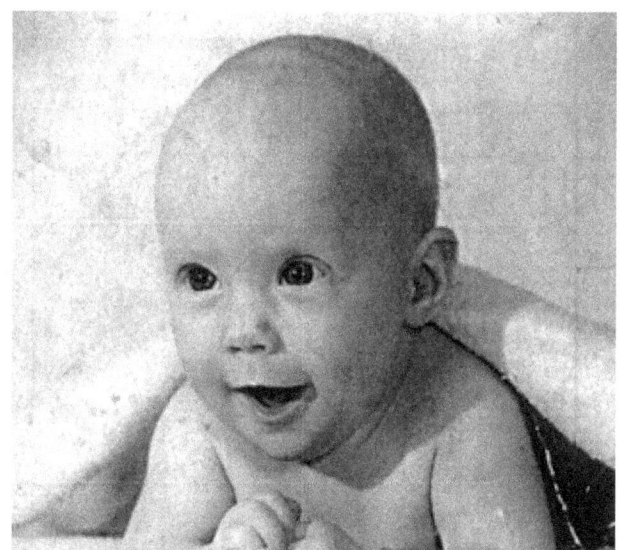
My first birthday

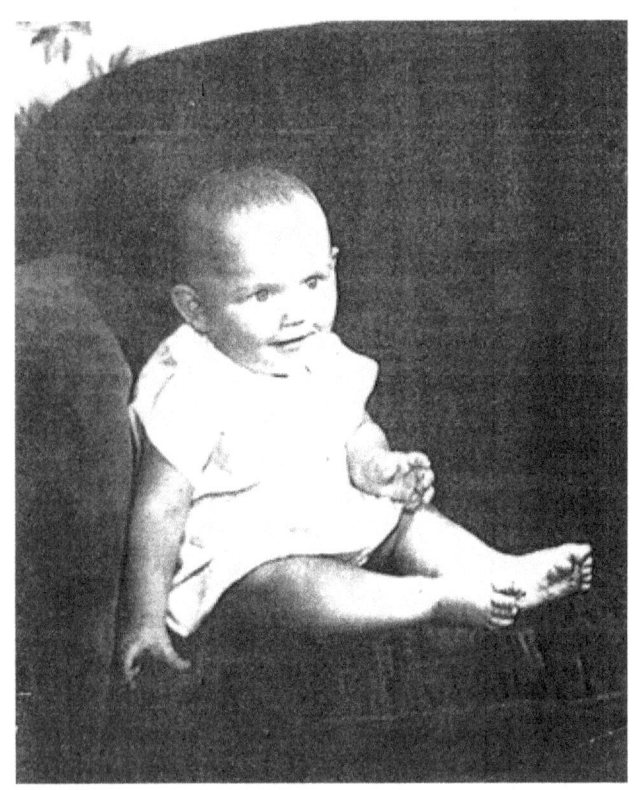

Me at three

Me at five

Me at twelve

Eulalie and me
Two different parties

www.ingramcontent.com/pod-product-compliance
Lightning Source LLC
Chambersburg PA
CBHW072022110526
44592CB00012B/1400